James L. Crenshaw

Prophetic Conflict

James L. Crenshaw

# Prophetic Conflict

## Its Effect Upon Israelite Religion

Walter de Gruyter · Berlin · New York
1971

Beiheft zur Zeitschrift für die alttestamentliche Wissenschaft

Herausgegeben von Georg Fohrer

124



ISBN 3 11 0033631



Printed in Germany

Satz und Druck: Walter de Gruyter & Co.

To Nita

*batăḥ bah leb bă'ᵉlah* (Prov 31 11a)

and

our sons, Tim and David

# Preface

J. Philip Hyatt and Walter Harrelson, two of my colleagues, and Martin Buss of Emory University were kind enough to read this manuscript and to offer many valuable suggestions for its improvement. To them I wish to express my deepest appreciation, for even when their suggestions were not followed, I have profited greatly from their insight into prophetic literature.

I wish also to express appreciation to the Research Councils of Mercer University and Vanderbilt University for generous grants enabling me to pursue this task with a minimum of distraction; to many students upon whom these ideas have been tested; and to Edith McGarrity for her cheerful and painstaking secretarial assistance.

Finally, I am particularly grateful to Professor Dr. Georg Fohrer for the inclusion of this study in the Beihefte to ZAW, and to my mother, who taught me to search the scriptures.

## Contents

# Abbreviations

| | |
|---|---|
| AJSL | American Journal of Semitic Languages |
| AndNQ | Andover Newton Quarterly |
| ANET | Ancient Near Eastern Texts Relating to the Old Testament, ed. J. Pritchard, 1955, 1969. |
| | |
| BEvTh | Beihefte to Evangelische Theologie |
| Bib | Biblica |
| BiOr | Bibliotheca Orientalis |
| BibSt | Biblische Studien |
| BJRL | Bulletin of the John Rylands Library |
| | |
| CBQ | Catholic Biblical Quarterly |
| | |
| Enc | Encounter |
| EstudEcles | Estudios Ecclesiasticos |
| EvTh | Evangelische Theologie |
| Exp | The Expositor |
| ExposT | The Expository Times |
| | |
| HO | Handbuch der Orientalistik |
| HThR | Harvard Theological Review |
| HUCA | Hebrew Union College Annual |
| | |
| IB | Interpreter's Bible |
| IDB | Interpreter's Dictionary of the Bible |
| Inter | Interpretation |
| | |
| JAAR | Journal of the American Academy of Religion |
| JB | Jerusalem Bible |
| JBL | Journal of Biblical Literature |
| JNES | Journal of Near Eastern Studies |
| JQR | Jewish Quarterly Review |
| JTS | Journal of Theological Studies |
| Jud | Judaica |
| | |
| LXX | Septuagint |
| | |
| ModR | Modern Review |

| | |
|---|---|
| OTS | Oudtestamentische Studiën |
| RA | Revue d'Assyriologie et d'Archéologie Orientale |
| RB | Revue Biblique |
| RefThR | The Reformed Theological Review |
| RGG | Die Religion in Geschichte und Gegenwart |
| RHPR | Revue d'Histoire et de Philosophie Religieuses |
| SEAJTh | South East Asia Journal of Theology |
| Sem | Semitics |
| STU | Schweizerische Theologische Umschau |
| SJTh | Scottish Journal of Theology |
| ThLZ | Theologische Literaturzeitung |
| ThR | Theologische Rundschau |
| ThSt | Theological Studies |
| ThVia | Theologia Viatorum |
| ThZ | Theologische Zeitschrift |
| TWNT | Theologisches Wörterbuch zum Neuem Testament, ed. G. Kittel |
| VT | Vetus Testamentum |
| VTS | Vetus Testamentum Supplements |
| WZJena | Wissenschaftliche Zeitschrift Jena |
| ZAS | Zeitschrift Ägyptologische Studien |
| ZAW | Zeitschrift für die alttestamentliche Wissenschaft |
| ZDPV | Zeitschrift des Deutschen Palästina-Vereins |
| ZSystTh | Zeitschrift für systematische Theologie |
| ZThK | Zeitschrift für Theologie und Kirche |

Would you that spangle of Existence spend
About the secret — quick about it, Friend!
A Hair perhaps divides the False and True —
And upon what, prithee, may Life depend?

A Hair perhaps divides the False and True;
Yes; and a single Alif were the clue —
Could you but find it — to the Treasure-house,
And peradventure to The Master too; . . .

The Rubaiyat of Omar Khayyam

INTRODUCTION

## Prophet versus Prophet

Prophetic literature testifies to lively conflict within the prophetic circle itself, thereby witnessing to the presence of diverse viewpoints within the group, and implying that prophetic inspiration was greatly affected by personal factors. In ten places the attack by one prophet upon another was so severe that the Septuagint translators used the word *pseudoprophētes* to translate *nabî'*. These refer to the future removal of every prophet and unclean spirit (Zech 13 2); accuse the prophets and priests of healing Israel's wound lightly, proclaiming peace when there is no peace (Jer 6 13); threaten the priests and prophets with death (Jer 26 7. 8. 11. 16); rebuke the prophets, diviners, dreamers, soothsayers, and sorcerers who are urging the Babylonian captives not to serve their conquerer (Jer 27 9); appeal to Israelites to disregard the "deceit and dreams" of the prophets and diviners who prophesy in Yahweh's name despite the fact that he has not sent them (Jer 29 1. 8), and identify Jeremiah's opponent Hananiah as a false spokesman of Yahweh (Jer 28 1).

The other passages in prophetic literature where prophets are attacked have a similar theme, even if the Septuagint translators did not use *pseudoprophētes* in these instances. The charge of immoral conduct appears in a few places, specifically drunkenness and adultery (Jer 23 11. 14. 30; cf. 28 7). In two passages the prophets persecute or seek to kill another prophet (I Kings 22 24 Jer 26 7ff.), while in another they are said to be insolent and treacherous (Zeph 3 4). The charge of theft is also made against these prophets, although the stolen object consists of "oracles" spoken by other prophets (Jer 14 14 23 16. 25ff.; cf. 29 8).

The usual charge, however, focuses upon the message, and is especially bitter. These prophets are accused of proclaiming lies (*šæqær*) and lying dreams (Jer 8 10 14 14 23 25. 32 27 10. 14. 16 28 15 29 9. 21), visions of their own heart (Ezek 13 1ff. 22 28 13 3), and peace (*šalôm*) when there is no peace (Ezek 13 10 Jer 6 14 8 11 14 13 23 17 28 2ff. 11 Mic 3 5ff.). Moreover, they are said to have been excluded from the council (*sôd*) of Yahweh (Jer 23 18)[1]; their divine commission is denied

[1] H. Wh. Robinson, The Council of Yahweh, JTS 45 (1944), 151—157; F. M. Cross, Jr., The Council of Yahweh in Second Isaiah, JNES 12 (1953), 274—277; E. C. Kingsbury, The Prophets and the Council of Yahweh, JBL 83 (1964), 276—286.

(Jer 29 8 f. 14 14 23 21 28 15 29 9 Ezek 13 6), and their source of inspiration and allegiance is attributed to Baal (Jer 2 8 5 31 23 13 32 32-35 Dtn 13 1ff. 18 20). Greed is also a charge, the prophets being accused of prophesying for money and coining the message according to the reward (Mic 3 5ff. 11 Ezek 13 19). Particularly damning is the accusation that they have failed to expose iniquity (Lam 2 4) and have attempted to cover up a grievous breach in the wall with whitewash (Ezek 13 10ff. 22 28-31), healing the wounds of the people lightly (Jer 6 13 f. 8 10).

Unique in the accounts of conflict within prophecy is Ezek 13 17-19, where prophetesses are accused of speaking their own thoughts and are attacked for sewing magic bands upon all wrists and making veils for the heads of persons of every size, hunting for souls. These magical practices are thought to have caused the death of blameless souls and preserved the life of guilty ones[2]. It is remarkable that prophetesses come under attack only in this passage, for at least two women are known to have belonged to the prophetic circles (Huldah [II Kings 22 14ff.] and the unnamed prophetess by whom Isaiah had the child named Maher-shalal-hash-baz [Isa 8 1-4]), and these passages do not imply that female prophecy is out of the ordinary[3].

This struggle within the ranks of prophecy itself, however bitter and fraught with consequences, was but one of several conflicts experienced by the prophets. As if constant battle with other prophetic spokesmen who saw things differently were not enough obstacle to the carrying out of the office of the prophet, there was also bitter fighting with the masses, whose view of reality often was in conflict

[2] G. Fohrer, Prophetie und Magie, ZAW 78 (1966), 25—47 (reprinted in: Studien zur alttestamentlichen Prophetie, 1967, 242—264), has called attention to magical elements within Israelite prophecy, providing a context within which to understand this passage from Ezekiel, as well as the related one in Dtn 18 9ff. Fohrer takes note of clairvoyant ability of some prophets and recognizes the magical element behind the idea of the effective power of prophetic word and symbolic action (31. 35f.), even if this word and deed stand in a dialectic relation to magic on account of Yahweh's sovereignty (40). The destruction of Baruch's scroll in Jer 36 Fohrer understands to be an attempt by Jehoiakim to neutralize the prophetic words of judgment (44f.), for the magical background of curses and woe oracles was taken for granted (37—44).

[3] Neh 6 10-14 mentions a prophetess named Noadiah, who assisted Shemaiah and other prophets in the attempt to lead Nehemiah to his death in the temple. The designation of Miriam (Ex 15 20) and Deborah (Judg 4 4) as prophetesses is, of course, to be understood from the perspective of a late desire to honor these women in the highest terms then available, just as Abraham (Gen 20 7), Moses (Dtn 34 10 18 15-22) and Aaron (Ex 7 1) are spoken of as prophets. The prominence of prophetesses in the service of Ishtar of Arbela and their presence at Mari suggest that female spokesmen for the gods have a long history in the ancient Near East.

with that of a particular prophet. Especially distasteful was this struggle when the prophetic predictions failed to materialize, proof positive to the people that the bearer of such a message was not sent by God and deserved death. Given this situation it is no surprise that still another struggle comes to the fore, namely that between a prophet and his Commissioner. The reasons for such "kicking at the pricks" were numerous; they extend from the failure of God to abide by his own word to the self-interest of a prophet for whom personal reputation for accuracy of proclamation is more important than the lives of a huge city. Between these extremes is the frequent struggle with God's decision to display his wrathful side, the prophet interceding for the doomed people and being urged to desist, and the agony over the injustice of God that appears to have broken many a life.

Such conflict inevitably led to self-interrogation, a situation far more agonizing than all the other battles. This inner struggle forced the prophet to ask whether the voice he "heard" was not the sound of thunder, the vision a nightmare. His answer may have been an arrogant boast that he alone possessed the power and spirit of God; a simple affirmation that the Lord took him; or a majestic account of a summons from the Lord, the Holy One of Israel. But regardless of his answer, the prophet could not escape the inner doubts forced upon him by the unbelieving populace, his disagreeing and often disagreeable colleagues, and a God who refused to be slave even to his own word.

In view of these facts, one must conclude that prophetic conflict is inevitable, growing out of the nature of prophecy itself. The prophetic function is best described as embodying four stages: (1) the secret experience with God, sometimes followed by ecstasy of concentration; (2) the prophet's interpretation of the unique experience according to the faith by which he lives; (3) the process of intellectual revision, particularly the addition of motivation clauses and conclusions; and (4) artistic development, the adaptation of the message to ancient rhetorical form and the clothing of it in metrical poetry[4]. Within the two-fold task of the reception of the word of God in the experience of divine mystery, and the articulation of that word to man in all its nuances and with persuasive cogency rest multiple possibilities for error and disbelief.

Furthermore, the likelihood of conflict within biblical prophecy is enhanced by the belief that Yahweh made use of men against their

[4] G. Fohrer, Introduction to the Old Testament, 1968, 349—350, where the dependence upon J. Hempel, Die althebräische Literatur und ihr hellenistisch-jüdisches Nachleben, 1930, is acknowledged. The subjective element in the total prophetic experience opens the way for human desires and ignorance as to the real purpose of God in human affairs.

will or knowledge to accomplish his intentions, indeed on occasion sent deceptive visions and devious words to further the divine purpose for Israel. In essence, then, human limitation and divine sovereignty combine to create tension within prophetic circles, so that a clarification of the conflict between prophets demands that attention be given to both factors. From such scrutiny it may be possible to clarify the issues between the prophet and his adversaries, to illuminate the prophetic mode of self-vindication, and to determine the effect of this struggle upon the history of Israelite religion.

CHAPTER I

# The Unfolding Drama of Research

## A. PROPHECY IN GENERAL

The history of prophetic research has undergone constant alternation between emphasis on the man and the message he proclaimed, the latter being dominant at present. The shift in emphasis over the past five decades is reflected quite vividly in the attempts of Eißfeldt, Wolff, Fohrer, and H. H. Schmid to analyze the major problems of prophetic research[1]. For Eißfeldt the basic issues were (1) cultic prophets; (2) the origin and transmission of prophetic books; and (3) the supranormal experiences of the prophets. Four years later Wolff could summarize the major problems confronting students of prophecy in terms of (1) the relationship between Israelite prophecy and that of the ancient Near East; (2) ecstasy; (3) the sacred traditions preserved by the prophets; (4) the cult; (5) the political role of prophets; and (6) false prophecy. The radical change is observable in Fohrer's article, although slightly different in kind, and that of Schmid, which is more directly comparable to those by Eißfeldt and Wolff. Fohrer's major concern is to correct erroneous assumptions and conclusions as to the traditions employed by the prophets, and to warn against too hasty "discovery" of new literary types. For Schmid the basic issues are (1) prophet and law; (2) prophet and office; and (3) prophet and wisdom. All of these belong to the broader heading of traditions employed by the prophets.

---

[1] O. Eißfeldt, The Prophetic Literature, The Old Testament and Modern Study, edited by H. H. Rowley, 1951, 115—161; H. W. Wolff, Hauptprobleme alttestamentlicher Prophetie, EvTh 15 (1955), 116—168, also in: Gesammelte Studien zum Alten Testament, 1964, 206—321; G. Fohrer, Remarks on Modern Interpretation of the Prophets, JBL 80 (1961), 309—319, reprinted in: Studien zur alttestamentlichen Prophetie (in German); and H. H. Schmid, Hauptprobleme der neueren Prophetenforschung, STU 35 (1965), 135—143. It is interesting to note that the prophetic literature itself (Former and Latter Prophets) bears witness to this changing emphasis. The older narratives focus upon the lives of the prophets, whereas classical prophecy stresses the content of the prophetic message, while exilic and post-exilic prophecy returns to a concern for the prophetic lives *as affected by opposition from their hearers*. This shift of emphasis has been perceived by R. Rendtorff, Men of God, 1968, 71.

The shift from the man to the message is clearly reflected in the literature under discussion, and grows out of the fact that careful study of the prophetic personality demands intimate knowledge of his oracles, and the total message reveals something about the character of the prophet himself. Indeed, at times it is difficult to determine whether person or message dominates the interest of an author, whether prophetic function or essence is being high-lighted. As a matter of fact, this ambiguity rests upon the failure of some prophets themselves to differentiate between their role and person (Jeremiah is particularly guilty of this confusion).

There is, however, a third factor that has not been given sufficient attention in prophetic research, namely the audience to whom the prophets spoke. The history of research both in the area of prophecy in general and in the more particular study of false prophecy appears to justify a movement in the direction of the people to whom the prophet was sent. In a very real sense much recent research has been studying the popular mind, since the traditions preserved by the people were taken up by prophets and used in the formation of an oracle. But a further step is essential, namely the analysis of the *vox populi* in ancient Israel[2]. We turn now to trace the history of prophetic research, hoping to justify the claim that the trend has been from man to message, and to reveal a distinct shift toward a study of popular religion.

## The Man

Before J. Wellhausen the prophet was understood as a preacher of the law promulgated by Moses, a system of legislation given to Israel by the God who had brought the nation into existence. But the revolutionary thesis popularized and cogently defended by Wellhausen that the law was subsequent to the prophets demanded a radical revision in the understanding of the function of prophecy. The prophets came to be regarded as the great originators of the noblest within Israelite religion, indeed were said to have introduced a universal view of history into Israel's faith. Wellhausen was convinced that great men live alone in the streams of world history; nowhere does this belief appear more poignantly than in the commemorative address Wellhausen delivered for his teacher, H. Ewald: "He died on May 4th, 1875, in conflict with the world, but in peace with God." For B. Duhm, too, the prophets were the really creative figures, reformers even, who

[2] For the recognition of the *vox populi* in the political situation of the ancient Near East, see S. N. Kramer, "Vox Populi" and the Sumerian Literary Documents, and P. Artzi, "Vox Populi" in the El-Amarna Tablets, RA 58 (1964), 149—156 and 159—166 respectively.

"set the relationship between God and people on a purely moral basis"[3].

This pronounced emphasis upon the personal experience and individuality of the prophet led to a study of the peculiar religious experience from which the prophet received his message. In 1914 G. Hölscher published his Die Profeten, an examination of the psychological aspects of prophetic experience. Hölscher claimed that all prophecy was ecstatic, and that ecstasy was Canaanite in origin. However, he contended that Israelite classical prophets refined the cultic religion into one of morality, that of nature into one of history. All subsequent studies of prophecy have been forced to deal with Hölscher's view of the primacy of ecstasy, and the psychological study of prophetic experience dominated the field for a quarter of a century. Such studies of Hosea and Ezekiel were made by A. Allwohn and K. Jaspers[4], while S. Mowinckel argued that the early prophets were moved by the Spirit (an alien force closely akin to pagan religious experience), whereas the later ones emphasized the word of the Lord[5]. Lindblom contributed immeasurably to this psychological study of prophecy by providing a definition of ecstasy, in which he distinguished between ecstasy of absorption and ecstasy of concentration. Nevertheless, Lindblom was able to discern the dangers of a onesided emphasis upon ecstasy, and issued an incisive caveat[6]. Despite this warning, however, the psychological study of prophecy and emphasis upon ecstasy was pressed to the limit by G. Widengren[7]. The limitations of the psychological approach to prophecy have been increasingly stressed, although few today would deny that genuine prophecy was ecstatic in the sense of absorption by one idea.

---

[3] For a detailed discussion of the contribution of these men, see W. Zimmerli, The Law and the Prophets, 1965, 17—30. This emphasis upon the individual is typical of the age, and can be observed as early as J. G. Herder and H. Ewald.

[4] A. Allwohn, Die Ehe des Propheten Hosea in psychoanalytischer Beleuchtung; and K. Jaspers, Der Prophet Ezechiel: Eine pathographische Studie, in: Arbeiten zur Psychiatrie (Festschrift für K. Schneider), 1947, 77ff. The extremes to which such study was taken can be seen in the article on Hosea's Motives by O. R. Sellers in AJSL 41 (1925), 243—247; and that by E. C. Broome on Ezekiel's Abnormal Personality, JBL 65 (1946), 277—292.

[5] The "Spirit" and the "Word" in the Pre-exilic Reforming Prophets, JBL 53 (1934), 199—227.

[6] Einige Grundfragen der alttestamentlichen Wissenschaft, in: A. Bertholet Festschrift, hrsg. W. Baumgartner und O. Eißfeldt (1950), 325—337; and Prophecy in Ancient Israel, 1962.

[7] Literary and Psychological Aspects of the Hebrew Prophets, 1948. A. Heschel, The Prophets, 1962, made a valuable contribution in this regard by calling attention to the prophetic participation in the divine pathos.

The research into the psychology of prophetic experience led to the study of the relationship between the classical prophets and the *nᵉbî'îm*, which raised the inevitable question of the cultic prophet. The first to perceive the existence of cultic prophecy was Mowinckel, who argued that the "prophetic oracles" in some of the psalms indicate that prophets were employed in the temple worship[8]. This cultic emphasis was taken up and advanced by a series of articles edited by S. H. Hooke[9], and by A. R. Johnson[10], A. Haldar[11] and I. Engnell[12].

The cult was also understood as the place where the prophetic word was preserved. H. S. Nyberg showed that the process of oral tradition had to be taken seriously[13], and Mowinckel gave the "circles of tradition" flesh and blood by pointing to the cultic disciples of prophets. H. Birkeland called attention to the place of oral tradition in the literature of Israel's neighbors[14], while E. Nielsen and A. H. J. Gunneweg drew many of the necessary conclusions following from the emphasis upon oral tradition[15]. A warning was tendered, however, by Widengren, who argued that writing was normative even in Arabic religious practice, oral tradition being of secondary significance[16]. Although the extreme positions of Haldar and Engnell are often criticized, few are willing to deny that genuine prophets were on occasion associated with the cult, and that this was a beneficial alliance. It has even been claimed that Joel, Habakkuk, Nahum, Zephaniah and Deutero-Isaiah are liturgies, although most scholars seem to think it is unlikely in each case but Habakkuk and perhaps Nahum[17].

---

[8] Psalmenstudien III: Die Kultprophetie und prophetische Psalmen, 1923. See also: The Psalms in Israel's Worship, 1962, 53—73.

[9] Myth, Ritual and Kingship, 1958; and The Labyrinth, 1935.

[10] The Cultic Prophet in Ancient Israel, 1944.

[11] Associations of Cult Prophets among the Ancient Semites, 1945.

[12] Profetia och Tradition, in: J. Lindblom Festschrift (1947), 110ff. (now in: A Rigid Scrutiny, translated and edited by J. T. Willis, 1969, 123—179); and The Call of Isaiah, An Exegetical and Comparative Study, 1949.

[13] Studien zum Hoseabuche, 1935.

[14] Zum hebräischen Traditionswesen, 1938.

[15] Oral Tradition, 1954; and Mündliche und schriftliche Tradition der vorexilischen Prophetenbücher als Problem der neueren Prophetenforschung, 1959. Gunneweg gives a very helpful survey of relevant literature.

[16] Widengren op. cit. passim.

[17] A. S. Kapelrud, Joel Studies, 1948; P. Humbert, Problèmes du livre d'Habacuc, 1944; A. Haldar, Studies in the Book of Nahum, 1947; G. Gerleman, Zephanja textkritisch und literarisch untersucht, 1942; and I. Engnell, The Ebed Yahweh Songs and the Suffering Messiah in Deutero-Isaiah, BJRL 31 (1948), 13ff. Wolff's observation that "cult and prophecy can no longer be spoken of as opposites; the cult of Israel is unthinkable without prophetic functionaries, as is prophecy of

If the prophet is understood as a cultic functionary, it is necessary that the prophetic office be clarified. Hence lively debate has come from the pens of a number of recent scholars. H. J. Kraus[18] and S. Mowinckel[19] suggested that there was an office of "Law Preacher", and that Moses is portrayed as such, a view that has recently claimed the attention of J. Muilenburg[20]. E. Würthwein attempted to show that Amos was an official of the cult and that he proclaimed the "amphictyonic" law[21], until the transition to a prophet of judgment[22]. R. Bach contended that in every instance Amos based his message upon the *apodictic laws*, while questioning the casuistic on occasion[23]. Würthwein then sought to show that not only ethical demands but also the preaching of judgment originated in the cult. To do so he "discovered" the origin of the *Gerichtsrede* in the cult[24], but was justifiably challenged in this thesis by F. Hesse, who objected to the use of Psalms and the hypothetical reconstruction of a ritual judgment enacted in the cult[25]. The most extensive analysis of the prophetic office has come from the research of H. Graf Reventlow, who has discussed Amos, Jeremiah and Ezekiel in terms of their prophetic office[26].

---

Israel without cultic traditions" appears to represent current thinking rather well (see Hauptprobleme alttestamentlicher Prophetie 225).

[18] Die prophetische Verkündigung des Rechts in Israel, 1957.

[19] Le Décalogue, 1927.

[20] The "Office" of the Prophet in Ancient Israel, in: The Bible in Modern Scholarship, edited by J. P. Hyatt, 1965, 74—97.

[21] The use of the word "amphictyony" is unfortunate, since the Tribal League does not meet the necessary requirements (central sanctuary, etc.) for such. This has been energetically emphasized recently by H. M. Orlinsky, The Tribal System of Israel and Related Groups in the Period of the Judges, Oriens Antiquus 1 (1962), 11—20; G. Fohrer, Altes Testament — "Amphiktyonie" und "Bund"?, ThLZ 91 (1966), 801—816. 893—904; and W. H. Irwin, Le sanctuaire central Israélite avant l'établissement de la monarchie, RB 72 (1965) 161—184.

[22] Amos-Studien, ZAW 62 (1949—50), 10—51. Fohrer's criticism of Würthwein's hypothesis in terms of the unity of 1 3—2 16; the crime of one foreign nation against another; the same period for all four visions; and the intercessory activity of non-cultic prophets is well taken (Introduction to the Old Testament 432).

[23] Gottesrecht und weltliches Recht in der Verkündigung des Propheten Amos, in: Festschrift für G. Dehn, 1957, 23—34.

[24] Der Ursprung der prophetischen Gerichtsrede, ZThK 49 (1952), 1—15.

[25] Wurzelt die prophetische Gerichtsrede im israelitischen Kult?, ZAW 65 (1953), 45—53.

[26] Das Amt des Propheten bei Amos, 1962; Liturgie und prophetisches Ich bei Jeremia, 1963; Wächter über Israel, Ezechiel und seine Tradition, 1962. See also Das Amt des Mazkir, ThZ 15 (1959), 161—175; and Prophetenamt und Mittleramt, ZThK 58 (1961), 269—284. J. Bright, Jeremiah's Complaints — Liturgy or Expression of Personal Distress? in: Proclamation and Presence (G. Henton Davies Festschrift,

The conflict between Amos and Amaziah, as well as Jeremiah's inner tension, are viewed as the conflict between two offices, and the constraint to prophesy in these men is said to arise from their office rather than a call from Yahweh. Reventlow thinks of the visions and oracles against the nations as ritual proclamation of the prophetic office and preaching of judgment during the covenant renewal. Moreover, Am 4 6-11 and 9 13-15 are viewed as rituals of blessing and cursing after the pattern of Lev 26. Ezekiel is also understood from the perspective of the prophetic office, the difference being that he is cut off from the sanctuary; however, both Ezekiel and Jeremiah are said to be watchmen over Israel and intercessors before God. The objections to these interpretations are numerous, but basically arise from Reventlow's failure to distinguish form and function, and the refusal to give sufficient weight to individuality among the prophets.

The study of cultic prophecy has also called attention to the political role of the prophet, especially the early *nᵉbî'îm*. But the classical prophets were often involved in the political situation, and this field of study has called forth treatments by E. Jenni, K. Elliger, H. J. Kraus, N. K. Gottwald and B. S. Childs[27]. The remarkable familiarity of the classical prophets with the major events of ancient Near Eastern history has been emphasized, together with the prophetic demand for faith in Yahweh's sovereignty over the affairs of human history. Moreover, the active participation of pre-classical prophets in *coup d'états* and the presence of court prophets indicate the significance of this area of study in illuminating both prophecy and the Israelite concept of kingship.

The cultic prophet was said to have been a spokesman for God to the people and for the people to God. The latter function has been the subject of special study by Hesse[28], and has been denied by H. W. Hertzberg[29]. The importance of the debate is immediately apparent when one notes the farreaching conclusions based on an assumption that intercession can only be practiced by a functionary of the cult, not by one who has genuine concern (cf. Würthwein on Amos, Reventlow on Jeremiah). The research done in the area of the prophetic

1970), 189—214, stoutly rejects Reventlow's thesis about the Confessions and the prophetic "I" in general.

[27] Die politischen Voraussagen der Propheten, 1965; Prophet und Politik, ZAW 53 (1935), 3ff.; Prophetie und Politik, Theologische Existenz heute 36 (1952), 41ff.; All the Kingdoms of the Earth, 1964; and Isaiah and the Assyrian Crisis, 1967, respectively. H. Donner, Israel unter den Völkern, 1964, may also be mentioned.

[28] Die Fürbitte im Alten Testament, 1951.

[29] Sind die Propheten Fürbitter?, in: Tradition und Situation (A. Weiser Festschrift, 1963), 63—74.

"office" led scholars into the pursuit of the material employed by the prophets, especially the traditions presupposed. Chief among those discussed are the legal and wisdom traditions.

## The Message

The speech forms deriving from the legal realm have been examined by Würthwein, H. J. Boecker, E. von Waldow and W. Zimmerli[30]. While Würthwein thinks the legal terminology (*Gerichtsrede*) derives from the cult, this has been challenged by Boecker, who calls attention to the thoroughly secular formulae derived from daily court life, and contends that the secular "law court" is the origin of the prophetic lawsuit. Von Waldow cut the Gordian knot, claiming that the form derives from the secular realm, the content (particularly the idea of Yahweh as judge and prosecuting attorney, which von Waldow derives from the idea of covenant faith where Yahweh is both covenant partner and guarantor of the covenant) from the cult. J. Harvey was convinced that the lawsuit owes its origin to international treaties[31], while D. R. Hillers argued that the prophets of Israel have based their messages upon ancient treaty-curses[32]. Neither author has satisfactorily dealt with the question, however, of the time lapse between the earlier treaties and Israelite prophecy, or suggested a reasonable explanation for the supposed influence, which is really less striking than thought, and falls into the category of common human experience rather than direct dependence of one culture upon another[33].

Other literary *Gattungen* were thought to have been extracted from the biblical text, chief of which are the divine *Selbsterweises* argued for by Zimmerli and the *Heilsorakel* by J. Begrich[34]. The rich

[30] Amos-Studien; Redeformen des israelitischen Rechtslebens, 1959; Der traditionsgeschichtliche Hintergrund der prophetischen Gerichtsreden, 1963; Ich bin Jahwe, in: Geschichte und Altes Testament (1953), 179—209, respectively.

[31] Le "Rîb-Pattern", Réquisitoire prophétique sur la rupture de l'alliance, Bib 43 (1962), 172—196.

[32] Treaty-Curses and the Old Testament Prophets, 1964.

[33] R. North, Angel-Prophet or Satan-Prophet, ZAW 82 (1970), 31—67, discusses the question as to whether the prophet is in his "core-function" a messenger or an advocate ("whether the core of prophetic utterance derives from a runner-function or a prosecutor-function", 64). North's treatment of the *rîb* literature is especially helpful; in the end he does not choose among the linking of the prophet-core to angel, satan or priest, but feels drawn to the view that "suzerainty-treaties simply borrowed a legal terminology from the same sources on which the prophets draw" (65).

[34] Das Wort des göttlichen Selbsterweises (Erweiswort), eine prophetische Gattung, in: Mélanges Bibliques rédigés en l'honneur de A. Robert, 1957, 154—164; and Das priesterliche Heilsorakel, ZAW 52 (1934), 81—92.

rewards of such form-critical study are seen in Westermann's recent treatment, *Basic Forms of Prophetic Speech*[35]. Central to the understanding of this book by Westermann is the view that the prophet was first and foremost a messenger. Such was the observation of Begrich in a masterful study of the speech forms of Deutero-Isaiah[36], and has been accepted as undeniable by recent scholars[37].

The prophetic texts from Mari testify to the prevalence of the understanding of the prophet as a messenger[38]. Despite the theological and socio-ethical differences between biblical prophecy and these texts, they are important for the present study in that they reveal that the problem of determining a genuine word of God existed in ancient Mari and that the content of these prophetic words was both weal and woe. Concern over validating a prophetic message is indicated by the sending of a lock of hair and hem of a garment to king Zimrilim (particularly important when a message was transmitted through an intermediary) and by the testing of a prophetic oracle at the hands of a haruspex[39]. Furthermore, these texts remind us by the combination of judgmental prophecy with promise of salvation that the biblical judgment prophets may "have made the description of their opponents, the salvation prophets, too one-sided"[40].

The wisdom tradition has also been mentioned as the source for much of the prophetic material. The first to argue that a particular prophet employed wisdom traditions was J. Fichtner, who thought of Isaiah as a one-time member of the Sages[41]. Lindblom then called attention to the presence of wisdom traditions within prophetic books, but refused to see the prophets as directly connected with the Sages[42]. However S. Terrien and Wolff have claimed that Amos made extensive use of wisdom material; indeed, Wolff thinks that the prophet's

[35] Published in 1967.

[36] Studien zu Deuterojesaja, 1963, originally published in 1938.

[37] Particularly J. F. Ross, The Prophet as Yahweh's Messenger, in: Israel's Prophetic Heritage, edited by B. W. Anderson and W. Harrelson, 1962, 98—107.

[38] Important literature is noted in C. Westermann, Basic Forms of Prophetic Speech, 215, n. 10; A. Malamat, VTS 15 (1966), 210 n. 1; and G. Fohrer, Zehn Jahre Literatur zur alttestamentlichen Prophetie, ThR 28 (1961—62), 306f. H. Schult, Vier weitere Mari-Briefe 'prophetischen' Inhalts, ZDPV 82 (1966), 228—232; W. L. Moran, New Evidence from Mari on the History of Prophecy, Bib 50 (1969), 15—56; and F. Ellermeier, Prophetie in Mari und Israel, 1968, should also be mentioned.

[39] Malamat, Prophetic Revelations in New Documents from Mari and the Bible, 225—226; and Moran op. cit. 21—24.

[40] Westerman, Basic Forms of Prophetic Speech, 127.

[41] Jesaja unter dem Weisen, ThLZ (1949), 75—80, reprinted in: Gottes Weisheit, 1965, 18—26. See also R. J. Anderson, Was Isaiah a Scribe ?, JBL 79 (1960), 57—58.

[42] Wisdom in the Old Testament Prophets, VTS 3 (1960), 192—204.

background is tribal wisdom[43], a thesis that has been challenged by the author[44] and questioned at points by G. Wanke[45] and H. H. Schmid[46]. The theophanic tradition and holy war have most revently been suggested as a more probable background for the prophet Amos[47], in many ways confirming R. Smend's incisive criticism of those who see that prophet as cultic[48]. The valuable contribution to our knowledge of holy war by von Rad deserves mention here, so much the more because he has been most insistent upon viewing the prophets as interpreters of sacral traditions[49], despite the sharp criticism by Fohrer[50].

In short, the study of the prophets has moved more and more in the direction of the popular traditions employed by the prophets, and in so doing, has returned to some of the insights of H. Gunkel, for whom the *vox populi* played a significant role. A comparable trend may be discerned in the study of false prophecy, to which we now turn.

## B. "FALSE" PROPHECY

It comes as no surprise that the understanding of false prophecy was greatly affected by the perspective from which prophecy itself was viewed, the changing approaches to the general phenomenon of prophecy being evident in the history of research into false prophecy. If one were to isolate two tendencies of the literature on false prophecy from this century, it would have to be the trend toward a denial of valid criteria for distinguishing the false from the true prophet, and the attempt to understand reasons for the phenomenon of false prophecy, particularly the human ingredient of all prophecy.

At the turn of the twentieth century a number of questions about false prophecy were yet unanswered. Does the mere lack of fulfillment of a prophetic word identify the speaker as a false prophet? Does prophetic participation as a cultic functionary automatically set the *Heilsnabi* off as a false spokesman? And related to that, does possession of the Spirit rather than the Word constitute a second-rate kind

[43] Amos and Wisdom, in: Israel's Prophetic Heritage, 108—115; and Amos' geistige Heimat, 1964, Dodekapropheton II Amos, 1969, respectively.

[44] The Influence of the Wise upon Amos, ZAW 78 (1967), 42—52.

[45] אוי und הוי, ZAW 78 (1966), 215—218.

[46] Hauptprobleme der neueren Prophetenforschung 142f.

[47] See the writer's Amos and the Theophanic Tradition, ZAW 80 (1968), 203—215.

[48] Das Nein des Amos, EvTh 23 (1963), 404—423.

[49] Old Testament Theology, II 1956; and Der Heilige Krieg im Alten Israel, 1958[3].

[50] Remarks on Modern Interpretation of the Prophets 314.

of prophecy? Does a false assessment of the historical situation, hence a giving of the wrong word for that hour, turn a true prophet into a false? In fact, is false prophecy a permanent state, and is its opposite also lasting, or can the true prophet become false and the false true? Is it ever possible to determine who is a false prophet; that is, did either another prophet or the populace have any means of identifying the false messenger, of denying that he had stood in the divine council? Again, was the prophet himself ever certain of his own status, or did he walk the razor's edge between certitude and doubt all his days? What were the obstacles to the faithful performance of one's prophetic ministry? Could an appropriate message for one day become inappropriate because of changed circumstances? Did prophets have direct access to God, so that false prophecy was any activity not based on immediacy with God? Have the views of false prophets been preserved in prophetic literature? These are the issues to which twentieth century students of false prophecy have addressed themselves, and although the problems have not been completely resolved, at least a partial resolution has taken place.

The problem posed by unfulfilled predictions came to the attention of J. Hempel[51], who recognized the contingent character of all prophecy and denied the validity of the criterion of fulfillment in distinguishing true from false prophecy. Hempel's basic thesis was that prophecy that failed to materialize was the occasion of new faith on the part of the prophet and his hearers, seen most clearly in Deutero-Isaiah. The two-fold problem of prophet versus the course of history and one prophecy versus another is evident in the great crisis in Israel's faith accompanying the fall of Jerusalem and murder of Gedaliah, a crisis all the more tragic because of prophets of weal and woe, each claiming divine authorization. The ministries of Isaiah and Jeremiah illustrate for Hempel the dual problem of the historical confirmation of prediction and faith against alien faith with equal certainty of its divine origin, the silence of Isaiah after the so-called Syro-Ephraimitic War being understood as the result of the failure of his word to find fulfillment in history, and the conflict between Jeremiah on the one hand and Hananiah, Ahab and Zedekiah on the other indicating the difficulty of the problem of discerning who spoke for Yahweh and who for himself alone. Deutero-Isaiah is said to have been particularly concerned with the non-fulfillment of prophecy inasmuch as he was convinced that Yahweh's word would not return until accomplishing its purpose, and this word for a captive people was one of grace, the forgiveness of sins, outpouring of the Spirit of the Lord, and emancipa-

[51] Vom irrenden Glauben, ZSystTh 7 (1930), 631—660, reprinted in: Apoxysmata, 1961, 174—197.

tion by Cyrus being viewed in eschatological terms with the original creation as the model. Hempel writes that Cyrus' failure to give Yahweh the credit for the victory over Babylon left Deutero-Isaiah standing in the lurch, with the result that this prophet proceeded to transform the Cyrus poem into a Servant Poem, the uniting factor being the twin ideas of compassion upon Israel and inclusion of the nations as objects of God's concern. Thus Hempel thinks that covenant mediator replaces Cyrus, the hope being the same but the form of its fulfillment different, and moves on to interpret the idea of the resurrection of the Servant as indicative of the Old Testament disparity between promise and fulfillment resolved in Jesus of Nazareth.

What Hempel perceived was the dynamic quality of a spoken word, the reality to be reckoned with in the community even if it did not materialize exactly in the manner expected. It was this "aliveness" of the spoken word and readiness of the prophet to adapt a previous word to a new situation that prompted him to deny that the lack of fulfillment of a prediction was in itself proof of false prophecy. But the first to wrestle with the problem of the cultic adaptation of traditional oracular material, indeed the whole issue of false prophecy and the cult, was G. von Rad[52], who even suggests that Deuteronomy is the product of the so-called false prophets. Central to von Rad's argument is the contention that false prophets delivered messages of well-being; he writes that from Micaiah to Ezekiel the problem is not social matters, the cult, the dogma of retribution, or the relation of foreigners to Yahweh, but rather the single issue of weal or woe[53]. Accordingly, Deuteronomy, which proclaims well-being based on the election love of Yahweh is said to have had in mind institutional prophecy when predicting a succession of prophets who would proclaim the bond between God and Israel. Von Rad notes that a word of weal is at home in Isaiah's message, and finds its advocates in Jeremiah's opponents and the antagonists of Micaiah. The thesis is even proposed that, whereas Jer 28 9 demands that the message of weal must be legitimated, Dtn 18 20-22 requires the validation of a judgmental word, since the genuine prophetic movement is understood to be institutional. Inasmuch as the cultic institution existed to mediate between man and God, intercession is said to have been essential to prophecy, even to such "individualists" as Jeremiah. Proof that Jeremiah's opponents were cultic officials is found in their emphasis upon the return of holy vessels and promise of peace *in this place*, that is the temple (Jer 14 13). Von Rad understands the old story in Num 11 24 ff. as a desire to legitimate cultic intercessors as Mosaic, but the fact that the

[52] Die falschen Propheten, ZAW 51 (1933), 109—120.
[53] Ibid. 112.

Spirit of Moses falls upon two men outside the tent indicates that free prophecy is also known and legitimated. The inclusion of Nahum in the literature deriving from the so-called false prophets is little surprise, for the affinity between this work and the prophecies of well-being is strong.

Now that cultic functionaries were thought to have been in some way vitally connected with the movement known as false prophecy the question emerged as to the relationship between possession of the Spirit and false prophecy, since ecstasy was thought to have characterized cultic prophecy, at least in its earliest stage. S. Mowinckel quickly voiced his opinion on this matter[54], suggesting that the pre-exilic reforming prophets thought in terms of the word of Yahweh rather than of possession by the Spirit, the emphasis of earlier *n^ebî'îm*. Despite the exceptional view expressed in I Kings 22, and various passages from later prophetic books which Mowinckel considers redactional glosses, it is argued that Ezekiel was a transitional figure, one who thinks in terms of the Spirit as a medium of inspiration and a motive principle transporting the prophet from place to place, while Deutero-Isaiah's affinity with the reforming prophets is underlined as well as Trito-Isaiah's acceptance of the Spirit as a prophetic endowment.

Mowinckel interprets passages that present a problem to his thesis in brilliant, if unconvincing, fashion. Hosea 9 7 is viewed as bitter scorn for the *n^ebî'îm* rather than quotation of criticism of Hosea; Mic 3 3-8 is seen as a rebuke of those who boast of Spirit possession; Jer 5 13 is taken as a pun directed against those who have no word, *n^ebî'îm* who will turn into wind (*rû^aḥ*); Isa 28 9-10 is interpreted as the prophet's caricature of the *n^ebî'îm* rather than popular mockery of Isaiah. Likewise, Isa 8 11 and Mic 2 6 are viewed as pneumatic vocabulary toned down, and the reformers are said to have changed the old formula used by seers, "the Spirit came upon me," to "Yahweh showed me, I saw Yahweh, heard him, the word of Yahweh came to me." But Mowinckel recognizes that the divine word may differ from that of the prophet, who may have received a word from demons; hence the moral and religious content of the word is said to prove its genuineness. It is noteworthy that Mowinckel thought of Ezekiel as a true ecstatic of the ancient type, but one who shared the reformers' moral and religious ideas, and post-exilic prophets are thought to have returned to the earlier *n^ebî'îm* for inspiration, although the language is merely traditional formulae.

Mowinckel's hypothesis called attention to a point that von Rad had raised in passing, namely that concern must be devoted to the

---

[54] The "Spirit" and the "Word" in the Pre-Exilic Reforming Prophets.

historical situation in which the prophet found himself. In this regard, the failure of post-exilic prophecy may be viewed as a refusal to recognize the changed historical circumstances, so that a reversion to pneumatic terminology inevitably failed. It was M. Buber[55] who perceived the significance of the historical moment for the prophetic word, and wrote that the correct interpretation of the historical times was the key to the distinction between true and false prophet, the latter being understood as a politician of illusion. Buber was astonished that a prophet with the conviction that he had been called before his birth to be a prophet to the nations would in the confrontation with Hananiah have a word but not the truth. The latter has been appropriately labeled a parrot of Isaiah, according to Buber, for he quotes the prophet without discerning that the times have changed radically. But Hananiah is given credit for believing in Yahweh as a God of principles, one who would stand by earlier promises, and for sincere patriotism, a quality that even Jeremiah admired. The true prophet, Buber proposed, is a realistic politician, one who views the total historical situation before formulating a message. Conversely, the false prophet is said to be one who has taken conditional promises and made them unconditional certainties for all time, hence preaching their own desires and living from dreams as if they were reality.

Now if a correct assessment of the historical situation is the prerequisite for prophecy, could a true prophet err in his evaluation of historical circumstances of a given moment and still remain true to his vocation, or would he automatically pass into the category of false prophet? The ease with which genuine prophecy became false and vice versa is the theme of a study by K. Harms[56], a book that is somewhat explainable in terms of the adverse circumstances under which it was written. Harms stresses the narrow boundary between the true and the false prophet, sees the origin of the latter in the divine counsel, and recognizes the unity of the Old and New Testaments at this point. The transition of true to false prophet is illustrated by Ezek 14 7-11, and explains the dubious character of Aaron, Gideon and the prophetic figures in I Kings 13. Harms thinks of Nathan as tottering on the brink when advising David to build the temple (II Sam 7 1 ff.) and of Jonah as moving in the direction of false prophecy when fleeing from the Lord and becoming angry because of His compassion for Nineveh. One lapse on the part of a true prophet is said to be sufficient to iden-

[55] Falsche Propheten, Die Wandlung 2 (1946—47), 277—283. Similarly T. W. Overholt, Jeremiah 27—29: The Question of False Prophecy, JAAR 35 (1967), 241—249, writes that "It is the historical context alone that makes an otherwise unobjectionable message 'false'" (245). Overholt notes that *the people* are the ones who need to discern whether a prophet is true or false (241).

[56] Die falschen Propheten: Eine biblische Untersuchung, 1947.

tify him with false prophecy (James 2 10), and a basic contributing factor to such lapse is the prophetic guild, for crowds increased the likelihood of a slip. Royal prophecy is also said to have been an aid to false prophecy, for true patriotism characterized this phenomenon (even if Jeremiah also had such feelings). Nevertheless, there is one point, according to Harms, where the fluid boundary between true and false prophecy disappears, namely the opposition between Yahwism and Baalism.

If the narrow line between true and false prophecy is difficult to walk, and if God himself is in some sense responsible for false prophecy, is there a single criterion that can be applied to every situation so that either the populace or another prophet can determine who has really stood in God's council *when He was not providing false words as a test?* This is the question that G. Quell raises[57], and the answer he arrives at is that only another prophet can distinguish the true from the false. The fact that prophecy operates on two levels, the human and the divine, that is, human beings acting in the service of God, rules out all witness to authenticity save the inner testimony of a genuine prophet, according to Quell. Therefore, he writes that the prophet can neither be judged theologically nor juridically, but only pneumatically, and we are reminded that all err on the way to truth. Quell even recognizes grades of difference among the true prophets, and discerns that the field of false prophecy is the distant past rather than the present. The divine role in false prophecy is admitted,especially in I Kings 22, Deutero-Isaiah, Job and Amos 3 16, while the difficulty of functioning as a prophet is said to have been depicted in the Confessions of Jeremiah, so that W. Staerk's truth criterion is impossible of application[58]. Quell admits that the divine commission cannot be proved, and can only be discerned by another prophet; the similarity with an ordeal where God provides the decision is emphasized, so that anyone who would set up a criterion to distinguish true from false prophecy would do well to raise for himself the three questions of Jer 23 23 f. Finally, Quell makes much of false prophecy as God's alien work, an instrument in the divine plan.

But if only another prophet can make a decision as to who is a genuine messenger of God, how does a prophet validate his ministry

---

[57] Wahre und falsche Propheten: Versuch einer Interpretation, 1952.

[58] Das Wahrheitskriterion der alttestamentlichen Prophetie, ZSystTh 5 (1928), 76–101. According to Staerk, the truth criterion is the inner testimony of the Holy Spirit that there is no prophetic message of judgment without the complement of salvation, and vice versa (83). In short, historical confirmation of a prophet's message legitimates the word of the genuine man of God (87). The truth criterion is said to have been operative in Isa 8 11ff. Mic 3 5ff. Dtn 18 21f. Zech 7 9f. Hab 1 13 Am 7 12ff. and Jer 28 1ff. 23 13—24 26.

to a sceptical public, and in what way does he gain personal assurance that he is not an instrument of God's alien work? This is the difficult problem claiming the attention of S. Blank[59], an issue forced upon him by the unwillingness of the contemporaries of the prophets to pay heed to the word of God, a fate awaiting most of the rabbinic students and ministers to whom these Goldensen lectures were first given. Blank saw the pronounced prophetic argumentation as a battle against the prophet's own uncertainties as well as against other opponents. Six arguments are said to have been used by Jeremiah in an attempt to assure people that God had sent him and to convince himself of that fact: (1) the fulfillment of predictions; (2) a simple affirmation; (3) the contrast with the *vox populi*; (4) the speaking of divine rather than human words; (5) the proof that the words are God's because true; and (6) the conformity of a message with God's nature. Blank views the call narrative as Jeremiah's diploma, and admits that the simple affirmation of 26 12-15 needs no supplement, for Jeremiah stood in God's private council (23 22), shared his moods (6 11 23 9), and was overcome with gloom. The argument from fulfillment is said to be least satisfying to Jeremiah, since it was little confort that a word of doom was fulfilled. Blank writes that Jeremiah's voice was clearly not that of the crowd, for he passed as a madman (29 26) and was a target for laughter (15 15 17 15 20 7 f.); indeed, only a fool would call down upon himself disaster, curses and flogging, would deliver a message that results in imprisonment and ostracism unless compelled to do so by God. Blank even sees the new covenant as a consequence of Jeremiah's quest for security, and the application of this prophet's arguments to the question of the authority of scripture as a whole is recognized.

The relationship of the prophet to his contemporaries is a theme taken up by E. Jacob[60] in an attempt to explain why some true prophets betrayed their calling, that is, to discuss in greater depth the transition from false to true prophecy that had come to the attention of K. Harms. Jacob points to four obstacles to true prophecy: (1) kingship, resulting in paid prophets who promoted royal interests; (2) tradition in terms of institution, messianism, nationalism; (3) the crowd, whose esteem was coveted by most prophets, and (4) the desire for success as confirmation of the prophetic ministry. The significance of I Kings 13 for the understanding of false prophecy is recognized by Jacob, for it shows the presence in all mediators of a germ of treason to their Lord. Jacob's thesis that true and false prophecy are not two

---

[59] Of a Truth the Lord Hath Sent Me: An Inquiry into the Source of the Prophet's Authority, 1955.

[60] Quelques remarques sur les faux prophètes, ThZ 13 (1957), 479—486.

separate camps, but that the latter is a constant temptation of the former grows out of a rejection of biblical criteria for distinguishing the one from the other. His desire to understand the reasons for false prophecy was a reminder that there are diversities of witnesses even to false prophecy.

The complexity of the phenomenon of false prophecy was emphasized by E. Osswald[61], who recognized the necessity of examining the prophetic literature case by case to determine the true from the false. Osswald was strongly influenced by von Rad's thesis expanded by Buber that the interpretation of the historical moment is decisive, although she also was inclined to believe that true prophets before the Babylonian exile preached woe almost exclusively. Some attention is given to false prophecy as an extra-Yahwistic problem, but the conclusion is reached that exclusive loyalty to Yahweh is the absolute norm of prophetic teaching. The various criteria traditionally put forward in determining true from false prophecy are submitted to exhaustive analysis, the conclusion being reached that no single criterion serves in every instance, so that a decision of faith is demanded. Osswald writes that "the true prophet must be able to distinguish whether a historical hour stands under the wrath or the love of God"[62].

The consideration of each incident involving so-called false prophets necessitates attention to the contexts within which prophetic conflict is described. Such is the method behind H. J. Kraus' study of prophecy in crisis[63]; here the author brings into sharp focus the conclusions reached in a thorough examination of the passages dealing with conflict between Jeremiah and other prophets by applying them to the larger question of true and false prophecy. Kraus emphasizes the variety of means by which the word of God comes to prophets (ecstasy, music and dance, glossolalia, dream, vision, audition) and the different kinds of prophets (ecstatic bands, individual seers, cultic and royal prophets). But the single factor that characterizes the genuine prophet is said to be an immediacy with God; the difference this immediate contact with the divine council makes is illustrated by I Kings 22, where the opponents of Micaiah are said to have been dependent upon the Spirit sent by Yahweh for their message. Genuine revelation, according to Kraus, comes directly from Yahweh to Micaiah, while false prophecy is mediated to the four hundred by the Spirit. This same point is said to rest behind Num 12 6-8, where it is claimed that Moses talked with God mouth to mouth, clearly and not in dark sayings, even beholding God's form, whereas ordinary proph-

[61] Falsche Prophetie im Alten Testament, 1962.

[62] Ibid. 22.

[63] Prophetie in der Krisis, Studien zu Texten aus dem Buch Jeremia, 1964.

ets are limited to visions and dreams. Micah 3 5 f. provides a third passage from which Kraus seeks to understand false prophecy; here the opponents of Micah are profoundly moved by the ancient election faith and covenant promises. Kraus concludes, therefore, that in none of these passages can we isolate prophetic figures deserving of the derogatory title "false prophets"[64]. Nevertheless, he does admit that real differences between true and false prophets exist, particularly the failure to proclaim the guilt of the people, to expose iniquity (Mic 3 8 Jer 23 17 Lam 2 14). This failure, Kraus contends, identifies the false prophet.

The attention to biblical context has prompted the question as to whether the views of false prophets have been preserved in prophetic literature. A. S. van der Woude[65] has attempted to discover additional information about false prophets by giving attention to disputations in Micah. Three passages come to his attention: (1) 2 6-11; (2) 4 9-14 5 4b-5; (3) 2 12-13 3 1ff. From these van der Woude concludes that false prophets were covenant-minded (both Zion and Sinai); used the title *mælæk* for Yahweh, thus saw him in terms of El of Ugarit; and looked upon the threat to Jerusalem as an occasion for a glorious defeat of their enemies who had dared to threaten Yahweh's covenant people. Van der Woude thus suggests that prophetic literature has faithfully preserved sayings by false prophets, often without the equivalents of quotation marks, and that much can be learned about the opponents of the "true" prophets by applying this assumption to other prophetic books[66].

Now that the study of conflict between prophets has been so productive in clarifying the situation out of which false prophecy emerged, it is time to press one step farther and take up the insight provided by H. W. Wolff and recently pursued by van der Woude that prophetic quotations are a veritable gold mine for information about the prophetic message and its impact. Indeed, the study of this material provides primary data about the obstacles confronted by prophets

---

[64] Ibid. 112.

[65] Micah in Dispute with the Pseudo-Prophets, VT 19 (1969), 244—260. E. Halpern, Hosea 2 1-3, a quotation from the words of False Prophets, Bet Miqra 11 (1965—66), 159—161, also argues for the presence of the views of false prophets within the prophetic canon. It is often contended that Nahum and Obadiah, and perhaps some of the oracles against foreign nations in Jer Ezek and Isa, represent literature from the false prophets.

[66] This brief survey is not intended to be exhaustive; rather its purpose has been to trace the major shifts in the research into false prophecy. Mention should be made, however, of the Vanderbilt Ph. D. Dissertation by E. Tilson on False Prophets in the Old Testament (1951), as well as the article on Prophet and Prophet by A. H. Edelkoort in OTS 5 (1948), 179—189.

and illuminates the thought-world of the masses to whom the prophets addressed themselves. Here one suddenly discovers the reasons for the crisis through which the ancient Israelites passed during the exilic and post-exilic period, the popular questioning of the justice of God that demanded some sort of response from the prophet beyond grandiose promise or threat of judgment in the future. In actuality, such a pursuit places the phenomenon of false prophecy in perspective by studying it against the backdrop of the decline of prophecy in ancient Israel due to the crisis of faith brought on by the denial of the justice of God. To look at the phenomenon of false prophecy against the background of the theological crisis in popular religion leading to the partial displacement of prophecy by wisdom and apocalyptic thinking is the intent of the present study.

CHAPTER II

# The Crisis of Faith

Van der Woude has observed in passing that we should study disputations in the prophetic literature of the pre-exilic period for knowledge about false prophecy, particularly those disputations with quotations[1]. His own description of the theology of false prophets is remarkably similar to that of C. J. Labuschagne, who has in mind the *vox populi* in eighth century Israel[2]. The present writer had concluded that the *vox populi* was crucial to the understanding of false prophecy and had undertaken the following analysis independently of either van der Woude or Labuschagne. However, a few words about their characterization of popular religion are in order.

According to Labuschagne popular theology was always opposed to prophetic, hence was a perversion of Yahwism "like a putrefaction transmuting one living cell after another"[3]. He notes that the perversion began as tacit permission of what should be opposed, became generally accepted in another generation, then traditional religion, and ultimately official, endorsed and taught by priests and prophets[4]. The anthropocentricity of popular religion is underscored, that is, the tendency to believe that the destructive qualities of Yahweh will only be used against the enemies of Israel despite her conduct. Labuschagne writes: "Entrenched in the spiritual bulwark of election and covenant, with a Yahweh watching over their interests and existence, the people felt secure, and with a Yahweh backing their cause, they lived complacently, knowing no disquietude"[5].

---

[1] Van der Woude op. cit. 246. R. Gordis, Quotations in Wisdom Literature, JQR 30 (1939), 123—147; Quotations in Oriental Literature, HUCA 22 (1949), 157—219; and The Book of God and Man, 1965, 169—189, makes much of quotations in ancient literature even when the equivalent of "quotation marks" is missing.

[2] Amos' Conception of God and the Popular Theology of his Time, in: Studies on the Books of Hosea and Amos, 1964—1965, 122—133. Labuschagne's Schriftprofetie en volksideologie, 1968, (not available to the author) continues the line of research suggested by the earlier article (see the summary by A. S. van der Woude in ZAW 81, 1969, 136).

[3] Amos' Conception of God and the Popular Theology of his Time 123.

[4] Ibid.

[5] Ibid. The message of Amos is seen as a challenge to this ease on Zion, for the roaring of the lion was no comforting sound, and *in Amos there was no pathos*.

Elsewhere Labuschagne has characterized this "paratheology" as ethnocentric, collectivistic at the expense of individual responsibility, and marked by certainty that Yahweh would only act for weal (except upon his enemies, that is, non-Israelites)[6]. This trust in God's saving deed was also emphasized by van der Woude, who noted that false prophets were covenant-minded, viewed Yahweh as *mælæk* in the sense of El, and engaged in *Realpolitik* rather than theology[7]. In neither of these authors does one discover any emphasis upon the positive aspects either of false prophets or of popular religion.

Few would question the essential accuracy of this description; however, it is only part of the truth. While Labuschagne thinks that the crisis caused by the fall of Samaria and Jerusalem placed two types of prophets at opposite poles (writing versus folk prophets), it must be noted that the conflict was present from the very beginning, as is evident in a study of quotations within prophetic literature. Once these expressions of popular theology are examined it becomes impossible to dismiss the *vox populi* as bad faith.

## A. VOX POPULI IN ANCIENT ISRAEL

Despite the fact that the study of literary forms is in a very real sense an analysis of the *vox populi*, what we have in mind is an examination of quotations of a viewpoint contrary to that of a "writing" prophet. It is only as one becomes familiar with the voice of the people that he can understand false prophecy, for *vox populi vox dei* is no novel concept[8].

The following will seek to show that the *vox populi* is characterized by: (1) confidence in God's faithfulness, (2) satisfaction with traditional religion, (3) defiance in the face of prophets who hold a different view, (4) despair when hope seems dead, (5) doubt as to the justice of God, and (6) historical pragmatism. We shall concentrate first upon the negative side of each of these perspectives, but their ambivalence will then be highlighted.

### *Confidence in God's Faithfulness*

Looked at from one perspective the confidence of the people is an expression of faith in the benevolence of God despite historical

[6] Schriftprofetie en volksideologie.

[7] Van der Woude op. cit. 255—260.

[8] Despite the appeal of the principle that there is no equitable government that is not the result of popular vote, Rousseau's famous dictum is limited by the fact that the voice of the people is often one growing out of fear and superstition.

circumstances, is in fact the kind of trust demanded of Ahaz by Isaiah (7 9). However, the confidence could also be divorced from either the moral context or the historical situation, thus becoming superstition. The ancient cultic cry "With us is God" was shouted from high place and sanctuary. As early as Amos the people had perverted the theological idea of election, had turned it into a cause for license rather than responsibility,

> "You only have I known of all the families of the earth;
> therefore I will punish you for all your iniquities" (3 2),

and had taken refuge in the hope of the theophany of Yahweh.

> "Seek good, and not evil,
> that you may live:
> and so the Lord, the God of Hosts,
> will be with you,
> *as you have said*" (5 14);
> "All the sinners of my people shall die by the sword,
> who say, 'Evil shall not overtake or meet us'" (9 10).

A similar situation is reflected in the books of Micah and Jeremiah. The former quotes the voice of his contemporaries in which their attitude to the true man of God is made manifest,

> "'Do not preach' — thus they preach —
> 'One should not preach of such things;
> disgrace will not overtake us'" (Mic 2 6),

and their confidence in Yahweh's goodness is sported despite their immoral conduct:

> "Its heads give judgment for a bribe,
> its priests teach for hire
> its prophets divine for money;
> yet they lean upon the Lord and say,
> 'Is not the Lord in the midst of us?
> No evil shall come upon us'" (Mic 3 11).

Jeremiah confronted a similar arrogant confidence in those who had disowned Yahweh, who were saying

> "They have spoken falsely of the Lord,
> and have said, 'He will do nothing;
> no evil will come upon us,
> nor shall we see sword or famine'" (5 12),

who were offering peace to those who went their own way

> "They say continually to those who despise the
> word of the Lord, 'It shall be well with you';
> and to every one who stubbornly follows his
> own heart, they say, 'No evil shall come upon you'" (23 17).

This same prophet was accused by the people of being unfair in proclaiming God's judgment to them

> "You say, 'I am innocent; surely his anger has
> turned from me.' Behold, I will bring you to
> judgment for saying, 'I have not sinned'" (2 35).

Jeremiah lashed out against the prophets who were saying to the people

> "... You shall not see the sword, nor shall you have
> famine, but I will give you assured peace in this place" (14 13b),

a word that Yahweh will soon force them and their hearers to eat (14 15-16). On that day the boastful words will be remembered

> "Behold, I am against you ... who say,
> 'Who shall come down against us, or who shall
> enter our habitations?'" (21 13).

The arrogance of the people can also be discerned in the content of oaths employed in Jeremiah's day. This is especially true of the popular "As the Lord lives who brought up the people of Israel out of the Land of Egypt" (23 7)[9]. Small wonder the people sucked confidence from the appeal to the ark (Jer 3 16), the temple (Jer 7 4. 10), and the possession of the law (Jer 8 8, "How can you say, 'We are wise, and the law of the Lord is with us'? But, behold, the false pen of the scribes has made it into a lie").

### *Satisfaction with Traditional Religion*

But the popular voice is also one of satisfaction with the status quo. The slowness of the people to respond, their hard-heartedness and blindness are nowhere better recognized than in Isaiah's report of his call (6 9-13). Here the function (even the purpose!) of the prophet is to "make the heart of this people fat, and their ears heavy, and shut their eyes; lest they see with their eyes, and hear with their ears, and understand with their hearts, and turn to be healed" (6 10). Such a ministry is vividly manifested in the encounter between the prophet and Ahaz (7 1-25). The king's pious response ("I will not ask, and I will not put the Lord to the test," 7 10) indicates that his eyes had been blinded more effectively than Zedekiah's at the hands of Nebuchadrezzar (II Kings 25 7).

---

[9] The evolution of the oath formula within ancient Israelite literature is discussed in the author's article *YHWH Ṣeba'ôt Šemô*: A Form-Critical Analysis, ZAW 80 (1969), 170f., where attention is called to oaths by pagan gods (Gen 14 19), by the life of Yahweh (Hos 4 15 Jer 4 1-2 5 1-3), by Yahweh as Israel's God (Josh 9 18), by Yahweh as redeemer (Jer 16 14 II Sam 4 9 15 21), and by Yahweh as Creator (Jer 38 16; cf. 32 22 Isa 54 9 65 16f.).

Isaiah was appalled by the corruption of the leaders of society, especially prophets and seers. He rebukes these men for their inability to perceive the simplest spiritual truth

> "And the vision of all this has become to you like the words of a book that is sealed. When men give it to one who can read, saying, 'Read this', he says, 'I cannot, for it is sealed'. And when they give the book to one who cannot read, saying 'Read this', he says, 'I cannot read'" (29 11-12).

The callousness of the people in Isaiah's day is summed up in the intriguing word of the prophet to the so-called good king Hezekiah and the response thereto (39 1-8). Despite the awesome prediction that Judah will be conquered, Jerusalem sacked and exiled, and Hezekiah's sons chosen to be eunuchs in the palace of the ruler of Babylon, Judah's king utters the incredible response

> "'The word of the Lord which you have spoken is good'. For he thought, 'There will be peace and security in my days'" (39 8).

Other prophets also confronted the spiritual lethargy of the people, and opposed it in equally vigorous language. Micah was convinced that a man who would invent a lie to the effect that he prophesies wine and strong drink would be a prophet for a people so insensitive to spiritual values (2 11). The prophet upon whom the immobility of the people grated most irritatingly seems to have been Jeremiah, who was especially sensitive to the opinions of the crowd. The adulation of wooden and stone images was particularly irksome, even if the religion of king, prince, priest and prophet.

> ". . . Who say to a tree, 'You are my father,'
> and to a stone, 'You gave me birth.'
> For they have turned their back to me,
> and not their face.
> But in the time of their trouble they say,
> 'Arise and save us!'" (2 27).

These contemporaries of Jeremiah had deluded themselves into thinking that their deeds were hidden from God, and the sins of the people caused both land and its inhabitants (birds and animals) to suffer, yet they said

> "He will not see our latter end" (12 4).

No wonder they warned the prophet not to prophesy in the name of Yahweh or he would die at their hands (11 21).

> "For I hear many whispering. Terror is on every side!
> 'Denounce him! Let us denounce him!'
> say all my familiar friends, watching for my fall.
> 'Perhaps he will be deceived, then we can overcome
> him, and take our revenge on him'" (20 10).

Jeremiah's contemporary, Ezekiel, likewise castigated the people for idolatrous worship and mental dullness. The first is the subject of a passage remarkably similar to Jer 12 4 (Ezek 8 12). After Ezekiel has looked through the divine periscope at the hidden practices of the Jerusalemites he is assured that their words are

> "The Lord does not see us, the Lord has
> forsaken the land" (8 12; cf. 9 9).

This prophet's contemporaries could not understand why the popular proverb that "the fathers have eaten sour grapes and the children's teeth are set on edge" had lost its value. Consequently, they objected "Why should not the son suffer for the iniquity of the father?" (18 19).

The books of Hosea and Zephaniah provide attestation to the existence of the *laissez faire* attitude during their ministries.

> "'The prophet is mad,' Israel protests,
> 'this inspired fellow is raving'" (Hos 9 7 JB).

To this popular rebuke Hosea responds with ringing poignancy

> "Ah yes, but only because your iniquity is so great,
> your apostasy so grave" (9 7 JB).

Zephaniah's contemporaries were convinced from their reading of current events that "the Lord will not do good, nor will he do ill" (1 12c).

### *Defiance*

The voice of the people is also one of defiance. This response to the prophet and the God for whom he spoke is evident in the books of Micah, Isaiah and Jeremiah. The prophet Micah was the object of the people's ire because of the apparent inactivity of God.

> "Then my enemy will see, and shame will
> cover her who said to me,
> 'Where is the Lord your God?'" (7 10)

The defiant mood reaches its zenith in Isaiah's contemporaries, Ephraimites who in arrogant pride have said

> "The bricks have fallen, but we will build
> with dressed stones;
> the sycamores have been cut down, but we will
> put cedars in their place" (9 10),

and in the inhabitants of Judah who ask

> "Who does he think he is lecturing? Who does
> he think his message is for? Babies just weaned?
> Babies just taken from the breast? With his
> *ṣăw laṣaw ṣăw laṣaw, qăw laqaw, qăw laqaw,*
> *zeʿer šam, zeʿer šam!*" (28 9-10 JB).

The mockery is in the form of infant babbling; Isaiah had become to them a plier of childish prattle, just as Ezekiel was thought to be one who spoke the language of pleasant love songs (33 32; cf. 20 49). The behavior of Isaiah's hearers is intentionally designed to thwart the purposes of the Holy One.

"Who say to the seers, 'See not'; and to the prophets, 'Prophesy not to us what is right; speak to us smooth things, prophesy illusions, leave the way, turn aside from the path, let us hear no more of the Holy One of Israel'" (30 10-11).

This same defiant spirit was encountered by the prophet from Anathoth, who speaks for Yahweh

"Have I been a wilderness to Israel,
or a land of thick darkness? Why then do my
people say, 'We are free, we will come no more to
thee'?" (Jer 2 31, cf. 6 16-17 22 21).

Yahweh's messenger also comes under attack because of the failure of the prophetic word to find effectual working out in the lives of the people. They taunt

"Where is the word of the Lord? Let it come!" (17 15).

*Despair*

Again, the voice of the people is one of despair. Jeremiah was keenly conscious of this element in the hearts of the people, whom he compared to a camel or an ass in heat whose desire for a mate could not be contained[10]. So those who had once worshipped other gods uttered resignedly

"It is hopeless, for I have loved strangers,
and after them I will go" (2 25b).

But this despair was not only the result of a propensity toward idolatry; it also arose from disappointment over unfulfilled prophetic predictions. What the people could not accept was the theological reality that the promise always exceeds the fulfillment, that religious man is often confronted with a famine in the land of promise[11]. So the cry rose to heaven

[10] K. E. Bailey and W. L. Holladay, The "Young Camel" and "Wild Ass" in Jer II 23-25, VT 18 (1968), 256—260, have pointed out that it is the male camel that experiences rut; accordingly the passage is understood somewhat differently on the basis of poetic structure.

[11] F. C. Fensham, Covenant, Promise, and Expectation in the Bible, ThZ 23 (1967), 305—322; C. Westermann, The Way of Promise through the Old Testament, in: The Old Testament and Christian Faith, edited by B. W. Anderson, 1963, 200—224, and Essays on Old Testament Hermeneutics, (editor) 1963, passim.

"Is the Lord not in Zion? Is her King not in her? . . .
The harvest is past, the summer is ended, and we
are not saved" (Jer 8 19-20).

Convinced that they had removed themselves from the possibility of forgiveness and transformation, these people turned their backs upon Jeremiah's plea for repentance

"But they say, 'That is in vain! We will follow our own plans, and will every one act according to the stubbornness of his evil heart'" (18 12).

The contemporaries of Isaiah were likewise convinced that there was a vast chasm between the prophetic promises of divine favor and the historical situation. Therefore, they rejected Isaiah's offer of heavenly aid in favor of more dependable means of deliverance from human foes.

"In returning and rest you shall be saved; in quietness and in trust shall be your strength. And you would not, but you said, 'No! We will speed upon horses,' therefore you shall speed away; and 'We will ride upon swift steeds,' therefore your pursuers shall be swift" (30 15-16).

### *Doubt as to God's Justice*

In the midst of this despair was an element of painful questioning of the sacred dogmas, an inquisitive spirit closely akin to the theodicies of Gen 18, Ex 32, Job, Habakkuk, and II Esdras. The claim that Yahweh was merciful, compassionate and slow to anger was questioned by the men of Jeremiah's day.

"Have you not just now called to me,
'My father, thou art the friend of my youth —
will he be angry for ever, will he be indignant to the end'" (3 4-5a)?

When these people are suffering from the punishment of God, their cry "Unfair" reaches the heavens (5 19).

Ezekiel's contemporaries dismissed him as irrelevant by their claim that his words concerned the remote future.

"Son of man, what is this proverb that you have about the land of Israel, saying, 'The days grow long, and every vision comes to nought'? . . . 'The vision that he sees is for many days hence, and he prophesies of times far off'" (Ezek 12 22. 27b).

These men also questioned the justice of God,

"Yet you say, 'The way of the Lord is not just'" (18 25),

although Ezekiel charged *them* with injustice and poor logic. Even as late as the post-exilic prophet Malachi the prophetic defense of God's justice had failed to convince the people. The experience of Job and the scepticism of Qoheleth had become all too common to dismiss as bad faith, although this is what Malachi does.

"You have wearied the Lord with your words. Yet you say, 'How have we wearied him?' By saying, 'Everyone who does evil is good in the sight of the Lord, and he delights in them.' Or by asking, 'Where is the God of justice?'"(2 17).

These people had recognized the falsity of the magical assumption in religion[12], and in reality had advanced beyond the spiritual perception of the prophet, although failing to draw the proper ethical conclusions. Their words are felt by Malachi as forceful

"Your words have been stout against me, says the Lord. Yet you say, 'How have we spoken against thee?' You have said, 'It is vain to serve God. What is the good of our keeping his charge or of walking as in mourning before the Lord of Hosts? Henceforth we deem the arrogant blessed; evildoers not only prosper but when they put God to the test they escape'" (3 12-15)[13].

## *Historical Pragmatism*

Lastly, the word of the people was one of historical pragmatism. The temper of such response to God and his action is set by the quotation in Isaiah 5 19,

"Let him make haste, let him speed his work that we may see it; let the purpose of the Holy One of Israel draw near, and let it come that we may know it!"

However, the *locus classicus* for such pragmatism is Jer 44 16-19.

"'As for the word which you have spoken to us in the name of the Lord, we will not listen to you. But we will do everything that we have vowed, burn incense to the queen of heaven and pour out libations to her, as we did, both we and our fathers, our kings and our princes, in the cities of Judah and in the streets of Jerusalem; for then we had plenty of food, and prospered, and saw no evil. But since we left off burning incense to the queen of heaven and pouring out libations to her, we have lacked everything and have been consumed by the sword and by famine.' And the women said, 'When we burned incense to the queen of heaven and poured out libations to her, was it without our husbands' approval that we made cakes for her bearing her image and poured out libations to her?'"

By way of contrast, the prophet Haggai used the pragmatic argument to indicate that economic hardship was directly attributable to sin

---

[12] E. M. Good, Irony in the Old Testament, 1965, 196—240, discusses the magical assumption in religion with keen insight.

[13] For discussion of this passage, see E. Pfeiffer, Die Disputationsworte im Buche Maleachi, EvTh 12 (1959), 546—568.

(1 5-11), indicating the weakness of this argument from either perspective[14].

In view of this examination of the *vox populi* in prophetic literature, a look at comparable sentiments in Deuteronomy and Psalms may be particularly illuminating. The quotations of popular expression in Deuteronomy are strikingly similar to those in prophecy. Dtn 1 27 accuses the Israelites of murmuring in their tents,

> "Because the Lord hated us he has brought us forth out of the land of Egypt, to give us into the hand of the Amorites, to destroy us."

Similarly, 9 28 depicts Moses as intercessor for Aaron and Israel after the construction of the golden calf, Moses' argument being

> "Lest the land from which thou didst bring us say, 'Because the Lord was not able to bring them into the land which he promised them, and because he hated them, he has brought them out to slay them in the wilderness.'"

In 4 6 the response of other peoples is also mentioned, this time the hypothetical utterance of amazement that

> "Surely this great nation is a wise and understanding people"

since they observe Yahweh's statutes. Quite different is 12 30, a warning against saying

> "How did these nations serve their gods? — That I also may do likewise."

Such a callous attitude is also attacked in 15 9 which recognizes the problems to be created by the year of release, and urges

> "Take heed lest there be a base thought in your heart, and you say, 'The seventh year, the year of release is near,' and your eye be hostile to your poor brother, and you give him nothing, and he cry to the Lord against you, and it be sin in you."

Again, 29 19 warns the one who, upon hearing the words of the sworn covenant, blesses himself and says within his heart,

> "I shall be safe, though I walk in the stubborness of my heart."

---

[14] This analysis of the *vox populi* does not claim to be exhaustive, inasmuch as Wolff has already dealt with the broader question of citations within prophetic literature. Rather an attempt has been made to select the most representative responses to the prophetic ministry and thereby to indicate the vast possibilities open to us. It is quite clear that the time has come for a comprehensive study of the religion of Israel that focuses upon popular rather than approved religion (that is, by those who wrote and edited the Old Testament). Something of the wealth of resources can be seen in the following popular expressions not treated above: (1) Am 6 10, "Hush! We must not mention the name of the Lord"; (2) Hos 10 3, "We have no king, for we fear not the Lord, and a king, what could he do for us?"; (3) Jer 2 6, "They did not say, 'Where is the Lord who brought us up from the land of Egypt . . .'?" (4) Isa 28 15, "We have made a covenant with death, and with Sheol we have an agreement; when the overwhelming scourge passes through it will not come to us; for we have made lies our refuge, and in falsehood we have taken shelter."

Finally, 31 17-18 contains a particularly poignant prediction that a day of woe will befall Israel, when she will say

> "Have not these evils come upon us
> because our God is not among us?"

and when God will surely hide his face from her because of the worship of idols.

The *vox populi* in Psalms has two foci, the railings of mocking enemies and the haunting questioning of God's justice. The enemies are described as thinking themselves unmovable (10 6), forgotten by God who has

> "hidden his face and will never see it" (10 11),

and beyond judgment (10 13). They think of their tongues as masters of the situation (12 4), and mock the devout one who has committed his soul to the care of the Lord (22 8). Their mockery,

> "Aha, Aha! our eyes have seen it! . . .
> Aha, we have our heart's desire!"

reveals their jubilance over the sorry lot of the righteous (35 21. 25 40 15 70 3). These wicked men eagerly await the death of their foe (41 5. 8), saying

> "God has forsaken him; pursue and seize him,
> for there is none to deliver him" (71 11).

The righteous are deemed vulnerable because of the absence of prophecy (74 8 f.), and the enemies of Israel plan to take possession of the pastures of God (83 4. 12).

These godless ones also question the justice of God, particularly because of his remoteness. The fool goes so far as to deny that there is a God (14 1), and the nations are likely to wonder about his presence (115 2 42 3. 10), although the man of faith asks if it is possible to escape his presence and answers

> "If I say, 'Let only darkness cover me, and the light about me be night', even the darkness is not dark to thee, the night is bright as the day; for darkness is light with thee" (139 11f.).

Consequently, he thinks that men must say

> "Surely there is a reward for the righteous;
> surely there is a God who judges on earth" (58 11).

The wicked who bellow with their mouths

> "Who will hear us?" (59 7)

are not so easily persuaded, however, for El Elyon dwells in the highest heaven, prompting the question

> "How can God know? Is there knowledge in the Most High?" (73 11).

Hence the evildoers slay the widow and the sojourner, and murder the fatherless, saying

"The Lord does not see;
the God of Jacob does not perceive" (94 7).

The other examples of the popular voice in Psalms are less significant, but may be mentioned. In 78 19 f. the incredulity of the Israelites during the wilderness wandering is cited:

"Can God spread a table in the wilderness? . . .
Can he also give bread, or provide meat for his people?"

Zion is the subject of the other passages, the first alluding to a record of those born in her (87 4. 5. 7), and the second recalling the mocking chants of the Babylonian captors

("Sing us one of the songs of Zion")

and the Edomites

("Rase it, rase it! Down to its foundations!" 137 3. 7).

The *vox populi* as described above has been formulated on the basis of the total impact of prophetic quotations of the popular mind. However, some of the citations are obvious creations of the prophets themselves, reflecting more the prophetic gift of mind reading than the actual voice of the people[15]. This is especially apparent in Isa 30 10 f., where the people are depicted as urging prophets to speak illusions, which really amounts to an interpretation of what is meant by the request that prophets speak *šalôm*, Jer 18 12, where the people are described as admitting the perversity of their hearts, and Dtn 29 19, which has a rebel admit his stubbornness[16]. Nevertheless, most of the quotations have a ring of authenticity that justifies their acceptance as genuine popular response to prophetic faith. This is also true when the word cited comes from "opposition prophets", for in these instances the *vox populi* cannot be distinguished from that of their favorite prophetic spokesmen (cf. Jer. 14 13b Mic 2 6).

The positive factor in the *vox populi* must not be ignored, for each of the six elements described above has a genuine place in Israel's theology. The confidence in God's faithfulness despite all evidence to the contrary is characteristic of the noblest moments in Israelite faith, particularly in the majestic theophanic hymn of Hab 3, but also in

[15] Von Rad, Old Testament Theology, II 75, writes that the prophets often caricatured the people. Such harsh characterization of the opponents of the prophets is seen in Isa 5 20 28 15 Jer 2 20. 25. 27 Am 2 12 Zeph 1 12.

[16] Wolff, Das Zitat im Prophetenspruch, 66—68, lists three criteria for determining the authenticity of a citation, namely (1) conformity to the historical situation (i. e., the probability criterion); (2) agreement with the manner of thinking of the one quoted; and (3) incomprehensibility (cf. Isa 28 9-13). Wolff also considers self-judgment as in Jer 2 20. 25 and Isa 28 15 unthinkable, and notes that the prophets often admit that their words are "in the hearts" of those quoted (cf. Zeph 1 12).

prophetic legend, where the young Hebrews vow to die for their faith even though their God could deliver them if he chose to do so (Dan 3 16-18). Such faith in God's goodness was often difficult to maintain, so that one must not disparage this conviction if it is based on the nature of God as compassionate (Dtn) and the election of Israel (II Isaiah). After all, the ancient word of comfort, "Fear not, for I am with thee" must have caused more consternation than solace, since Israel's history seldom witnessed to such divine presence[17].

Similarly, there is a grain of truth in the people's satisfaction with the status quo, for it represented a conservative stance that recognized the worth of ancient (Mosaic) traditions, and demanded that change be justified. The people's apparent dullness and failure to comprehend the simplest spiritual realities is partly the fault of the prophets themselves, for the latter were not free of "whining grudge"[18] and vindictiveness, were not masters of the art of pedagogy or communication when self-esteem was at stake. Even the defiant spirit cannot be decried, since on occasion both the prophet and his Commissioner were guilty of attitudes unworthy of each (the intercession for Israel by Moses and for Sodom and Gomorrah by Abraham are examples of Promethean defiance few would condemn).

Can it also be argued that despair played a positive role in Israelite religion? Even if one refuses, as he must, I think, to resort to the argument that despair forced the Israelite to look at the bright prospects of the grace of God (now made known in the New Covenant), he can praise for their honesty those who gave vent to their hopelessness, and perchance admire them for the refusal to accept an authoritative word that did not validate itself in some convincing manner (a life of love!)

The same may be said of those who questioned the justice of God, particularly on the basis of historical circumstances, and who complained when their virtue was not rewarded. It was precisely this kind of heroism that erupted in the book of Job, for the dogma of individual retribution was positively criminal in its effect, even if based on the assumption that the Creator fashioned the universe so that accord with the principle of justice was rewarded.

---

[17] H. D. Preuss, "... ich will mit dir sein!", ZAW 80 (1968), 139—173, discusses this formula for divine guidance in terms of the nomadic idea of a deity who shepherds and protects his people. One must ask whether the "battle" context is given sufficient consideration in this helpful essay, however.

[18] North, Angel-Prophet or Satan-Prophet, 53, uses this phrase in distinguishing Jeremiah's complaints from the milder disputations in Malachi. C. Westermann, Propheten, in: Biblisch-Historisches Handwörterbuch, III 1966, 1511, observes that the disputes in Malachi indicate a transition of prophecy to teaching, inasmuch as the opposition to the prophet is taken up into the prophetic word. Accordingly, these disputations are genuine teaching rather than self-vindication of the prophet.

Finally, it should be noted that anthropocentricity is far from the evil Labuschagne would make it out to be. On the contrary, the orientation of wisdom literature is basically anthropocentric, as Zimmerli has demonstrated[19], and much of the prophetic literature at its highest peaks is almost solely anthropocentric (Mic 3 6-8 Am 5 24 f.). Even the ethnocentricity must be understood in terms of the mission of Israel to bless mankind and be a light to the nations (Gen 12 1ff. Isa 49 6), and the collective thinking typical of early Israel was indispensable both from the societal and the religious viewpoint. In brief, while Labuschagne and van der Woude have assisted greatly in clarifying the negative facet of popular religion, there is another side that should not be neglected, one that illuminates the conflict between prophets in wondrous fashion.

## B. THE QUESTION OF THE JUSTICE OF GOD

It has been argued above that the *vox populi* called into question the justice of God; since it is often said that Job was an attack on popular religion, a few observations are in order[20]. The dogma of individual retribution, far from being a concoction of the egocentric populace, was coined by the religious leaders of Israel. Prophet, priest and sage contributed to the popularity of the dogma, so that one must conclude that the doctrine of individual retribution was endorsed by institutional religion. Prophecy's covenantal and "holy war" traditions, indeed its fundamental premise that God controlled history, support the view that virtue is rewarded. Similarly, the legal and magical background of priestly religion belongs to the thought-world of those who, on the crassest level, assume that the deity repays those who contribute to his well-being by sacrifice or conduct. And, of course, the presupposition of wisdom throughout the ancient Near East is that God has created the universe in such a way that it will automatically reward those who abide by the principle by which the-world coheres (*ma'at, ME, ṣedaqa*)[21]. Into such a world-view the principle of grace fits poorly, and one can see the tension between the two comprehensions of divine attitude in all three strata of biblical literature.

The kinship between popular views and those expressed in Job can be illustrated by an analysis of prophetic disputations where the justice of God comes under attack. The mood of the people is set by

[19] Zur Struktur der alttestamentlichen Weisheit, ZAW 51 (1933), 177—204 ("What is good/profitable *for man*?").

[20] For fuller discussion see the author's Popular Questioning of the Justice of God in Ancient Israel, ZAW 82 (1970), 380—395.

[21] H. Schmid, Gerechtigkeit als Weltordnung, 1968.

Ezekiel, who quotes them as saying that every vision comes to nothing so that one is forced to conclude that God's way is not just (Ezek 12 22 18 21). Of the six discussions analyzed by E. Pfeiffer in Malachi, two question the justice of God (2 17—3 5 3 13-21 [Eng. 3 13—4 3])[22]. In Isa 29 15 f. we find another dispute in which the prophet attempts to defend the justice of God by accusing the people of arrogating to themselves the prerogatives of deity. To make his point Isaiah uses a *Streitfabel*[23], according to which the absurdity of a reversal of roles by the potter and the clay is called to their attention.

Mic 2 6-11 opens with the quotation of popular reaction to the prophet, probably the oracles of opposing prophetic spokesmen (but the viewpoint is clearly that of the masses), then moves into a defense of the justice of God in terms of his patience and Israel's guilt, and concludes with a caricature of the message desired by the people. Another passage that can be illuminated best by seeing it against the background of the question of theodicy is Isa 28 23-29. Here the appeal to a hearing gives way to questions about procedures in successful farming, interrupted by the claim that such tactics are taught to the farmer by God. There follows further description of the farmer's activity, both in declarative and interrogative form, appropriately brought to a conclusion by a doxology praising God for his wonderful counsel and excellent wisdom. Isa 40 27-31 also belongs to this context, for here one discovers the opening question and quotation ("Why do you say ..., 'My way is hid from the Lord, and my right is disregarded by my God'?"), together with hymnic praise and promise of future bliss. Grounds for such hope are found in the knowledge that Yahweh is Creator, unsearchable in understanding and gracious in caring for the weak. In short, when one discerns the frequency with which the justice of God is questioned in the *vox populi*, on the one hand, and the institutional preservation of the belief in individual retribution, on the other, it becomes impossible to view Job as an attack on popular religion.

But the recognition that the *vox populi* and Job speak with the same voice must not cause us to overlook the fact that the questioning of God's justice is one of the primary concerns of wisdom literature throughout the ancient Near East[24]. Basically three answers were

---

[22] Die Disputationsworte im Buche Maleachi.

[23] H. Gressmann, Israels Spruchweisheit in Zusammenhang der Weltliteratur, 1925, 28f., uses this term to describe Isa 10 15, a similar passage. The differences between these two verses and genuine fables is so great, however, that the term must be used with caution.

[24] Pritchard, ANET, 405—410. 434—440; W. G. Lambert, Babylonian Wisdom Literature, 1960, 21—91. 139—149; S. N. Kramer, Man and his God: A Sumerian Variation of the "Job" Motif, SVT 3 (1960), 170—182.

given to the problem posed by the apparent injustice of the gods: (1) human beings are innately evil, so that whatever their lot it is less odious than they deserve; (2) the gods are unjust; and (3) man's knowledge is partial, since the gods are hidden. All three responses may be seen in the Israelite attempts to wrestle with the problem, namely Gen 18, Ex 32, Hab, Job, Qoheleth and II Esdras. In these one can discern a growing tendency to draw out the implications of the third answer, particularly in the notion of suffering as disciplinary and final resolution of the problem after death.

In conclusion, what has this study of the *vox populi* and questioning of God's justice taught us? In the first place, it has pointed to the ambivalence of popular religion. No longer will it be possible to view the religion of the people as unambiguously corrupt, thus constituting a handy foil against which to look at the pristine prophetic faith. Once this fact is grasped, it forces us to re-examine the theology of "false prophets", inasmuch as their orientation is frequently similar to the popular religion discussed above. This second look at so-called false prophecy may illuminate the reasons for prophetic conflict, particularly if the opposing views are understood to possess a degree of truth.

Second, the crisis of faith in ancient Israel stems from the Achilles-heel of ancient prophecy, namely the absence of any validation for a prophetic word. The prophet was particularly vulnerable since he claimed to speak what another had communicated to him, yet when challenged as to the source of his word, he could only affirm that God had indeed summoned him, sent the vision, spoken the word. Given the absence of any convincing means of self-validation, one should not be astonished to discover that the prophetic interpretation of history as the arena in which God moved and over which he had ultimate control was contested, particularly when collective thinking began to give way to a quasi-individualistic stance[25]. We shall have more to say about this later, but first it is necessary to examine the means by which a prophetic spokesman sought to validate his word to hostile audiences. The failure of all criteria for distinguishing the true from the false prophet is depicted in the prophetic legend (midrash?) of I Kings 13, to which we now turn.

[25] S. B. Frost, The Death of Josiah: A Conspiracy of Silence, JBL 87 (1968), 369—382, has called attention to the strange failure of the Old Testament to deal with the one event that contradicted the basic thesis of prophetic theology (indeed the faith of the whole Old Testament, 377), namely the death of Josiah. Frost writes: "The fact is that the death of Josiah proved to be the relatively small but sharp-edged rock on which the OT concept of divinely motivated history foundered" (381).

CHAPTER III

# Prophecy's Inability to Face the Challenge

## A. I KINGS 13—A PERSPECTIVE ON PROPHETIC CONFLICT

### *1. Exposition of I Kings 13*

K. Barth has called I Kings 13 "perhaps the most expressive and at any rate the richest and most comprehensive prophetic story in the Old Testament"[1]. The narrative may be briefly summarized as follows. Having established royal sanctuaries at Bethel and Dan, and having appointed a special feast as the occasion for sacrificing upon the altars, Jeroboam went up to Bethel for the purpose of offering incense. A man of God from Judah, obedient to the word of the Lord, prophesied against the altar, predicting its desecration. The irate king stretched forth his hand, ordering the seizure of the prophet, only to have it stricken with leprosy and to provoke a sign from the man of God, namely the tearing down of the altar and scattering of the ashes. Jeroboam pleads for healing, receives his hand whole again, and shows gratitude by inviting the man of God to his home for refreshing and a reward. The invitation is spurned, however, on the basis that the Lord had specifically forbidden the man of God to eat bread or drink water in Bethel and had instructed him to return to Judah by a different route from the one he had traversed on the journey to Bethel.

The news of this happening and the prophecy was conveyed to an aged *nabî'* in Bethel. This prophet ordered his sons to saddle an ass for him, and went in pursuit of the man of God, finding him under "the oak". Having made certain of the identity of the man, the *nabî'* invited him to a meal, only to receive the same response earlier given to Jeroboam. The *nabî'* appealed to the fact that he too was a prophet, and that an angel had commanded him to bring back the man of God for a meal. This lie was convincing, and the meal commenced.

Again the word of the Lord came, this time to the *nabî'*, who cried out that this disobedience on the part of the man of God would result in a burial outside his ancestral grave. The condemned man of God went his way, only to be slain by a lion; the body was not eaten,

[1] Church Dogmatics, II 2, 1957, 409; the exegesis of I Kings 13 is reprinted in: BibSt 10 (1955), 12—56.

however, the lion standing aloof from man and ass. Passersby beheld this strange sight, and conveyed word to the inhabitants of Bethel. Whereupon the old *nabî'* went to the site, gathered up the body of the man of God, and returned to Bethel. Burial of the disobedient one followed, he being put to rest in the personal grave of the old *nabî'*, who requested that his own sons bury him beside the man of God, for the prophecy about the altar of Bethel "and against all the houses of the high places which are in the cities of Samaria" would surely come to pass. But Jeroboam remained unchanged!

## Barth's Classic Treatment

Barth's exegesis of this story has been called one of the finest examples of biblical interpretation in the last fifty years[2]. According to him the narrative concerns the polarities of divine election and rejection, combining in remarkable fashion the tension between the nation and the individual. The contrasts are striking: the independent man of God versus the professional prophet, the nation Judah versus Israel. The question at issue is the possibility of fellowship between Bethel and Jerusalem. Barth calls attention to three crises in the story: (1) one word of God against another word of God, 11-19; (2) the proclamation from the mouth of a liar of the authentic word of God, a message of condemnation, 20-26; and (3) the old *nabî'* seeking a refuge beside the dead man's bones, 27-32. Two pictures stand out with special clarity, the man of God behind whom stands the Davidic king Josiah, and the professional prophet under the sponsorship of the pro-Canaanite Jeroboam. The first proclaims that the cause of Yahweh is irresistible, carried out by a professional *nabî'* when the man of God proves unfaithful. It further recognizes that even the chosen ones, Jerusalem and the Davidic monarchy, will be false to the Lord. The second picture portrays Samaria as the temptress responsible for the Canaanization of Judah, and suggests that Yahweh is nonetheless remarkably patient with Ephraim, even sending prophets to them and permitting the guilty professional to go free while punishing the man of God for a single transgression of a secondary injunction. The juxtaposition of the two pictures suggests that Judah and Israel cannot live in isolation, but must remain in dialogue, an addressing of the rejected by the elect one. The real epilogue is recognized as II Kings 23 15-20, the story of Josiah's destruction of the sanctuaries and leaving untouched the bones of the man of God and the old *nabî'*, and the sum and sub-

---

[2] M. A. Klopfenstein, I Könige 13, in: ΠΑΡΡΗΣΙΑ, K. Barth zum achtzigsten Geburtstag, 1966, 639. M. Noth, Könige, 1968, 306f., calls attention to some necessary correctives of Barth's interpretation.

stance of I Kings 13 is said to be the message of Isa 40 8, "The Word of God endures forever"[3].

From this brief account of Barth's analysis of the narrative it can be readily seen that Klopfenstein's estimate, though somewhat exaggerated, is essentially correct. Nevertheless, Barth's interpretation was only a pointer to the way, as Klopfenstein rightly perceives, for the narrative is not really concerned with election and rejection. Therefore, much remains to be said about the brief narrative, and to the accomplishment of this we now turn.

## Further Clarification

It has been recognized that the section beginning at 12 32 and ending at 13 32 is a secondary insertion not to be ascribed to the Deuteronomic compiler, for 13 34 links with 12 31[4]. Two divisions of the material commend themselves, 12 32—13 10 and 13 11-32[5]. The story itself belongs to the literary category of a prophetic legend, although the form is generally written about a famous prophet and comes from late literature[6]. There is a kernel of historical fact in the story, however; but the specification of this continuum is fraught with difficulty. Noth conjectures a local Bethel tradition dating from after Josiah's reform of the cult[7], while J. A. Montgomery and H. S. Gehman think in terms of a legend that developed to explain the untimely end of some holy man[8].

The man of God from Judah is unnamed, but Wellhausen rightly saw the influence of the Amos narrative upon the story[9]. Even if we follow later scholars and add as prophetic prototypes Hosea, Elisha, Micaiah and Ahijah (with Klopfenstein), still the kinship with the Amos story is striking and calls for further discussion.

A list of the points of contact would include the following items: (1) both are from Judah, and in obedience to the word of the Lord

---

[3] Barth, Church Dogmatics, 393—409.

[4] O. Eißfeldt, The Old Testament, an Introduction, 1965, 290; A. Weiser, The Old Testament: Its Formation and Development, 1961, 178 (post-Deuteronomic appendices probably).

[5] M. Noth, Könige, 291. J. Gray, I and II Kings, A Commentary, 1963, 293, thinks in terms of 12 32—13 6 and 13 7-32.

[6] A. Bentzen, Introduction to the Old Testament, 1959, 237—240, has described this genre most helpfully.

[7] M. Noth, Überlieferungsgeschichtliche Studien, 1957, 79 note 3; 81. 97.

[8] The Book of Kings, 1951, 262.

[9] A recent discussion (not available to the author) of popular ideas about Amos is the article entitled: Amos und Jona in volkstümlicher Überlieferung by O. Eißfeldt in: Barnikol Festschrift, 1964, 9—13.

appear in Bethel and prophesy the destruction of the altar; (2) both have a run-in with Jeroboam, either personally or in the form of a priestly official; (3) "eating bread" plays a role in both ministries; (4) a lion plays a prominent part in both accounts. Other points of possible correspondence are: (1) Jeroboam could not return his hand; could this possibly rest behind the enigmatic expression "I will not cause it to return"? (Am 1 3. 6. 9. 11. 13 2 1. 4. 6); (2) there is a question as to whether either Amos or the man of God from Judah was a *nabî'*; (3) was the old *nabî'* a false prophet with malevolent intention, and was Amaziah's purpose an evil one? (Am 7 10-17)[10]; (4) can the reference to bodies cast out in silence in Amos echo the body cast out in this story? (8 3).

But some striking differences occur, and must not be overlooked: (1) Amos gives no portents; (2) nor did he concern himself with *impure* altars; (3) Amos was urged to eat bread *in Judah* (earn his living or stay alive?); (4) Amos was opposed by a priest; (5) Jeroboam is in the background in the book of Amos.

Despite these differences the probability is that Amos is the prophet behind I Kings 13. If so, where was the story preserved, in Bethel or in Judah? The careful avoidance of the title *nabî'* (with but a single exception) to designate the man of God, and the insistence upon calling the southern prophet a man of God and the prophet from Bethel a *nabî'* could have different purposes according to its northern or southern provenance. If the story comes from Bethel, this may be a derogatory term, the man of God referring to one whose authority is dependent upon the possession of the charisma, whereas the *nabî'* is an official, and thus legitimate, prophet. On the other hand, if preserved in Judah, the avoidance of the term *nabî'* may grow out of a suspicion that cultic prophets are not genuinely proclaiming the word of the Lord. The story as it now stands certainly represents a bias in favor of the man of God from Judah, chiefly accomplished by the addition of the phrase "he lied to him"[11]. However, it is probable that the story originally circulated at Bethel, and reflects a northern perspective.

A number of factors have led most scholars to view the narrative as late, chief of which are (1) the anonymity of the man of God and *nabî'*; (2) the mention of an angel as the mediator of revelation (not the "angel of Yahweh"); (3) the didactic *Tendenz*; (4) the magical remnants; (5) the presence of the holy man who works miracles even

---

[10] Würthwein, Amos-Studien, has argued that Amaziah was kindly disposed toward Amos, but this is not likely in view of the prophet's response to him.

[11] Quell, Wahre und falsche Propheten: Versuch einer Interpretation, 70 note 2, thinks that Šanda may be right that "he lied to him" is a gloss.

after death; (6) the folkloristic behavior of the lion; (7) the mention of Josiah by name; (8) the reference to the cities of Samaria, impossible before 734 B.C.; and (9) the mechanical view of prophecy and its validation.

Few of these arguments are compelling. Anonymity is no proof of lateness, indeed, it could point to just the reverse. Nor is didacticism peculiar to the late literature, for as early as Amos the didactic style of the wise was employed (3 3-8). The same can be said of the magical elements, for prophetic symbolism rests on magic as its base, and the Elisha narrative also contains the element of a holy man working wonders after death (cf. also the old Balaam narrative). Likewise this cycle speaks of bears that punish the mocking children of Bethel (II Kings 2 23-25). Finally, the mechanical view of prophecy is basic to Deuteronomy (13). There still remain, however, the decisive mention of Josiah, which C. F. Keil's attempt to interpret as an appellative ("He whom Yahweh supports")[12] does not remove, the allusion to an angel as the mediator of a word from God, (but see I Kings 19 5 and note the fact that the second word of Yahweh comes without angelic mediation) and the reference to the cities of Samaria.

These factors suggest that an old oral tradition about a man of God who confronted Jeroboam with a pronouncement concerning the desecration of the altar of Bethel and who rejected the king's hospitality has been added by the Deuteronomic compiler (or perhaps a subsequent editor) after Josiah's reform, the occasion of the accidental discovery and intentional preservation of the grave alluded to in the tradition.

The purpose of the story is debated[13], although the reason for its inclusion in the Deuteronomic history seems to be clear. The narrative points out that Jeroboam had ample warning from a genuine man of God, thus magnifying his guilt[14]. This is a much more adequate view than the thesis of Montgomery and Gehman that the story intends to teach a moral about the disobedient prophet[15], for the man of God is pictured favorably in the narrative, as the request by the *nabî'* to be buried beside his bones indicates.

Several points of the story deserve further attention, especially the anonymity of the prophet, the motive of the old *nabî'*, the role of

---

[12] C. F. Keil, The Book of Kings, (no date), 206ff.

[13] J. Lindblom, Prophecy in Ancient Israel, 63f., suggests that the story circulated because it provided a precedent in how to solve the problem of determining a genuine revelation from a false, namely when one you received is contradicted by that of another, trust yours. It is unlikely, however, that such advice was necessary given man's innate religious arrogance!

[14] N. H. Snaith, I and II Kings, IB 1954, 120.

[15] The Book of Kings 261.

the lion, and the four sharp contrasts appearing in the account. First, the ancient tradition as to the identity of the man of God. In II Chr 13 22 a prophet named Iddo is mentioned, it being claimed that the deeds and words of Abijah are recorded in the story of the prophet Iddo. Josephus (Ant. VIII, 9,1) names the man of God Yadon, which may be borrowed from II Chr 13 22[16].

The reason for the old *nabî*'s unusual behavior has been variously interpreted, depending upon whether with Šanda one follows the Septuagint in omitting the phrase (*kiḥeš lô*) "he lied to him" (13 18). The absence of *waw* is strange, but may be explained by haplography, so that a final decision cannot be made. Consequently the opinions about the old *nabî*' are both favorable and unfavorable. C. F. Keil championed the thesis that the *nabî*' was an honorable prophet in the employ of Yahweh[17], a view espoused recently by Klopfenstein, who goes so far as to argue that the syncretistic cult of Jeroboam was a legitimate form of Yahweh worship[18]. Those who view the *nabî*' from another perspective understand his action as prompted by a sinister motive or a desire to enhance his own prestige. They rightly observe that when the man of God spurned the king's invitation he was calling into question the legitimacy of the cult sponsored by the king. However the further assumption that the *nabî*' and his sons were professional cultic prophets employed by Jeroboam is not borne out in the text. On the other hand, if the *nabî*' merely wishes to gain status by association with the wonder-working man of God, the lie is understandable, as is the request about the burial of his corpse, which may be an attempt to make amends for a wrong done the man of God, or may simply be a testimony to the genuineness of the latter's ministry. The authenticity of the *nabî*'s word cannot be denied on the basis of the reference to an angel, for this motif is found in Ezekiel and Zechariah, not to mention the Elohistic narrative. The angelic mediation of the word may be a theological device to relieve the divine responsibility for the sinister invitation, that is, to account for the false message[19]. Finally, lest it be overlooked, the covenantal character of the meal is basic to this narrative, so that the invitation is less innocuous than would otherwise appear[20].

---

[16] Gray, I and II Kings, 295f. *Ya'adôn*, by metathesis *'idôn*; but Gray also thinks *'iddô* can be a common noun rather than a name, since *'ôded* appears for soothsayers or prophets in the inscriptions of Zakir of Hamath and of *La'ash*.

[17] The Book of the Kings 206—207.

[18] I Könige 13, 658.

[19] Montgomery and Gehman, The Books of Kings, 261, and Snaith, I and II Kings, 122.

[20] Gray, I and II Kings, 297, surmises that the invitation by Jeroboam is to a meal in the sanctuary dining hall.

One of the most fascinating elements of the story is the role of the lion, which Barth considers important in view of Gen 49 9 Am 1 2 3 8[21]. Lions were abundant in Israel in the earliest days and again after the Assyrians depopulated the area, as can be seen in the enigmatic account in II Kings 17 25 f. Here the gentiles settled by Sargon in Samaria are plagued by lions, a situation interpreted as God's punishment upon them for failing to observe the law of the god of the land, until a priest is sent to teach them proper fear of the Lord. But the most suggestive passage is I Kings 20 35-43. In this account a professional prophet asks a fellow guildsman to strike him, only to be refused. He then tells the disobedient son of a prophet that a lion will kill him as soon as he departs, a prophecy that promptly came true. The next time, the *nabî'* was succesful in getting a fellow to smite him, and with bandaged face confronted Ahab, tricking the king into pronouncing his own death sentence.

H. Gressmann's discussion of the narrative in I Kings 13 in terms of "The disobedient man of God and God's obedient animal" is well known[22], as is W. Vischer's statement to the effect that here is "a shadow of the lion that Amos heard roaring from Zion"[23]. Klopfenstein has correctly observed that the lion is a symbol for the king, and watches over the sanctuary, hence is a servant of the king[24]. The frequency of the metaphor for Yahweh has long been noted (Am 1 2 Jer 25 30 Joel 4 16 Hos 5 14 13 7 f.)[25].

The four sharp contrasts in the narrative stand out with unforgettable clarity. Here we see standing over against one another a lone man of God and a professional *nabî'*, Judah and Israel, Josiah and Jeroboam, God and man. The irony of the story is that each demands his counterpart, that none is capable of turning his back upon his

---

[21] Church Dogmatics 397. But see the remarks by Noth, Könige, 302, warning against spiritualizing this incident.

[22] Die Heilige Schrift des Alten Testaments, II 1923, 243.

[23] Das Christuszeugnis des Alten Testaments I 356 (The Witness of the Old Testament to Christ, 1949). For discussion of the lion in Egypt, see Emma Brunner-Traut, Altägyptische Tiergeschichte und Fabel. Gestalt und Strahlkraft, Saeculum 1 (1959), 124—185.

[24] I Könige 13, 663. The role of the lion in Assyrian ideology is too well known to demand additional comment, save to call attention to the appropriateness of the language employed by Nahum.

[25] For discussion of metaphors descriptive of Yahweh, see Hempel, Jahwegleichnisse der israelitischen Propheten, ZAW 42 (1924), 74—104, and for the relationship of God, man and animals: Gott, Mensch und Tier im Alten Testament, ZSystTh 9 (1931), 211—249, both reprinted in: Apoxysmata. It is no accident that the description of Yahweh in terms of a bull was avoided in Israel, particularly in view of the prominence of this idea in Canaanite literature (but note *'abîr ya'ᵃqob*).

opposite. The man of God must witness to the rejected one, for only by going North with his word can he confirm and justify his own election. "The true Israel must converse with the false Israel just because it is not a stranger to the latter's guilt ..."[26]. So also the *nabî'* must proclaim the word of Yahweh when the man of God proves unfaithful, and the sin and punishment of the latter has not altered his mission, his value, or his superiority over the prophet from Bethel[27].

## *2. Observations about the Study of False Prophecy*

### Two Mutually Exclusive Words Claiming Divine Origin

The significance of I Kings 13 for a study of false prophecy has hitherto been largely overlooked as the decisive key to the understanding of prophetic aberrance. Here the prophet from Bethel voices a claim to prophecy on a par with that of the man of God from Judah. "I also am a prophet as you are" (v. 18). Herein lies the problem to which this study is addressed — the claim and/or conviction on the part of so-called "false prophets" that they are exercising a genuine prophetic ministry. The difficulty with this claim or conviction is vividly illustrated in the confrontation between the man of God from the South and the prophet of Yahweh from the North, an incident in which both men claimed to possess a word from God, although the words were mutually exclusive. Is it possible that both men are prophets in the employ of Yahweh, and that the appellation "false prophet" is of no value in this context? And if this be the case in I Kings 13, can it also be true of other similar claims on the part of prophets whose message and conduct differed from those of the usual stripe of prophecy in the Old Testament?

### Massoretic Text Has no Term for False Prophet

An indication of the inappropriateness of the title "false prophet" may be discovered in the fact that the Massoretic Text has no such word, here or elsewhere, it having entered the Old Testament by way of the Septuagint, where one finds some form of *pseudoprophḗtes* ten times[28]. E. Jacob has underscored the radical difference between the

[26] Barth, Church Dogmatics, 404. The guilt of both kingdoms is portrayed most vividly by Ezekiel, who compares Jerusalem and Samaria to two harlotrous sisters, each trying to outdo the other in profligacy (23 1-49).

[27] Ibid. 397.

[28] Zech 13 2 Jer 6 13 33 7. 8. 11. 16 34 9 35 1 36 1. 8 (MT, 26 7. 8. 11. 16 27 9 28 1 29 1. 8 6 13). G. von Rad, Die falschen Propheten, 109, has recognized the significance of the absence of a Hebrew term for false prophet, and has indicated the additional difficulty of understanding the phenomenon deriving from this omission.

assertion within the Hebrew text that these prophets spoke falsehood or vanity (*šæqær or šaw'*) and the Greek word[29], for the Hebrew words refer to the *content of the prophetic message* whereas the Greek term focuses upon the *character of the prophet.* Even if the Massoretic Text had no special word for the false prophet, however, it did usually reserve the titles seer (*ro'æ* and *ḥozæ*), servant of God (*'æbæd 'ælohîm*), man of God (*'îš 'ælohîm*)[30], for those who have come to be known as prophets[31]. Moreover, the "false prophets" were frequently called (or linked with) diviners and mediums, so that the absence of a word for false prophet does not mean that the concept was entirely missing from ancient Israel, even if most texts simply use the word "prophet" for the "false prophet". Rather it signifies that the phenomenon of "false prophecy" was vastly more complex than the Septuagint would lead one to believe.

## No Valid Criterion

At the outset it must be declared that this passage deals the death knell to every attempt to specify absolute criteria by which to differentiate the true from the false prophet, for the ultimate criterion to

---

[29] Quelques remarques sur les faux prophètes 479. That the speeches against the prophets in Jer 23 9-40 and Ezek 13 1-23 are editorially linked has long been recognized (S. Mowinckel, Prophecy and Tradition, 1946, 50; von Rad, Old Testament Theology, II 40; and Lindblom, Prophecy in Ancient Israel, 153, where Ezekiel's speech against the prophets is even called a fictitious one). The basic Hebrew terms in these speeches are *šaw', šæqær, qæsæm, 'awæn, šalôm* and *sôd.* The first two refer to the deceitful nature of the messages proclaimed by these prophets, hence their worthless, vain and false character. The next two, *qæsæm* and *'awæn,* point to the divinatory and magical quality of the messages, and link the prophet quite closely with the priest and ancient seer. The use of *šalôm* to describe the prophetic message identifies the prophet with the cult and its purpose of promoting the well-being of the people of God, while the denial that the false prophets have stood in Yahweh's *sôd* is tantamount to accusing them of no immediacy with God, the pre-requisite for prophecy. For a helpful treatment of *šalôm,* see von Rad's article in TWNT II, 402—406, and for the idea of Yahweh's council, E. C. Kingsbury, The Prophets and the Council of Yahweh, JBL 83 (1964), 279—286; and Whedbee, Isaiah and Wisdom, Chapter IV (see also footnote 1 of the Introduction).

[30] Lindblom, Prophecy in Ancient Israel, 61, emphasizes the fact that *'îš YHWH* (man of *Yahweh*) never occurs. For a helpful discussion of the "man of God" in the Old Testament, particularly his wonder-working power and interest in nature rather than history, see C. Westermann, Propheten, 1499f.

[31] Harms, Die falschen Propheten: Eine biblische Untersuchung, 10; and Siegman, The False Prophets of the Old Testament, 1939, 2. Against this, however, is the Balaam narrative (see below), the biblical tradition being divided as to whether this prophet is to be numbered among the true or false messengers of God.

which contemporary scholarship appeals (the charismatic intuition of a true prophet)[32] fails in this instance.

## Narrow Line Between True and False Prophecy

Not only does I Kings 13 set the stage for the present discussion in that it provides an example of two mutually exclusive words claiming divine origin and an incident in which there is no specific word for false prophet employed, as well as one where no valid criterion between true and false prophecy exists, but the passage also depicts the narrow line between true and false prophecy in graphic terms. In Barth's words, the man of God shows "the abyss on whose edge ... every man of God and every genuine prophet walks"[33]. Here one sees the true prophet become false to his commission, and the "false prophet" take up the genuine word of God and let it fall with shattering force upon the erring man of God.

## Divine Causality

Finally, I Kings 13 points to the divine causality as the explanation of the phenomenon known as false prophecy. In this instance the element of testing comes to the fore, and approaches the demonic. Approaches the demonic, but does not quite reach it, for the Old Testament witness to the divine benevolence can not be pushed aside. The story illustrates the mysterious working (alien work) of the Sovereign Lord, the Creator who shapes the history of the people of God by every means available to him within the relationship of the covenant between free man and a self-limiting deity.

However, before turning to an analysis of the criteria for distinguishing a true from a false prophet, it may be helpful to ask which prophetic figure in this chapter represents popular religion as described above. Perhaps such a question is unanswerable, but a few observations may not be out of place. The aged *nabî'* from Bethel appears to fit into the category of the false prophet delineated by van der Woude, that is, one whose overarching concern is *Realpolitik,* who emphasizes Yahweh's kingship, and who is persuaded that the covenant relation assures the people of divine protection. But even these conclusions are extremely tenuous owing to the nature of the text, which is terribly enigmatic. At least it can be said without fear of contradiction that

[32] Quell, Wahre und falsche Propheten: Versuch einer Interpretation, 206. This would be true if the additional criterion favored by E. Osswald, Falsche Prophetie im Alten Testament, 22—23, be accepted, for the false prophet in this instance proclaims judgment rather than weal.

[33] Church Dogmatics 399.

the king had nothing but scorn for a prophetic word of doom and contempt for its bearer until needing his intercession. Finally, if the meal to which the man of God was invited really were cultic, then a further word could be said about the nature of the religion represented by the old *nabî'*.

## B. THE LACK OF A VALID CRITERION

The setting up of criteria for the separation of true from false prophets is as old as the conflict between prophets[34]. Although many in number, these criteria may be divided into two categories: those focusing upon the message and those concerning themselves with the man[35].

### *1. Message-centered Criteria*

The emphasis upon the prophetic message assumes four forms: (1) the fulfillment or non-fulfillment of the prophecy; (2) the promise of weal or woe; (3) the revelatory form (ecstasy or non-ecstatic experience; dream or vision; spirit or word); and (4) the undivided allegiance to Yahweh or apostasy from Yahweh to Baal.

#### Fulfillment or Non-fulfillment

Perhaps the most frequently employed criterion in the Old Testament is that of fulfillment or non-fulfillment. The author of Deutero-

[34] Quell, Wahre und falsche Propheten: Versuch einer Interpretation, 214f., reminds all who would set up criteria to distinguish true from false prophets that the three questions in Jer 23 23f. are imperative. Origen's observation that "it is not so when one speaks as a prophet he is a prophet, but when one is a prophet he speaks as a prophet" provides a helpful stance from which to approach the general problem before us. Note also the late M. Noth's observation: "For all historical phenomena, if they are really to belong to human history, must be ambiguous; and it does not become easy to differentiate between the true and the false by applying merely superficial criteria" (History and the Word of God in the Old Testament, in: The Laws in the Pentateuch and Other Essays, 1966, 192).

[35] Scott, The Relevance of the Prophets, 93—99, thinks in terms of (1) psychological, (2) rational, and (3) moral criteria. In the first he includes inner constraint, clarity and power of utterance; in the second, consistency with the original commission and Yahweh's will as made known in past prophetic utterances, while immediate relevance is associated with the third. R. E. Clements, Prophecy and Covenant, 1965, 127, writes that the falseness of a prophetic oracle could be detected by lack of conformity to historical events, to the Yahwistic tradition, or to a genuine prophetic oracle.

nomy uses this standard as if it were irrefutable: "When a prophet speaks in the name of the Lord, if the word does not come to pass or come true, that is a word which the Lord has not spoken ..." (18 22). Likewise the Deuteronomic historian has Micaiah ben Imlah subject his own message and that of his opponents to this criterion: "If you return in peace, the Lord has not spoken by me" (I Kings 22 28). Again the prophet Isaiah requests that his words be inscribed in a book for a witness in the time to come, that is, as a permanent means of testing the fulfillment or non-fulfillment of his words (Isa 30 8). The point is made even more forcefully by Ezekiel: "When this comes — and come it will! — then they will know that a prophet has been among them" (33 33). The same may be said of Jeremiah's classic statement on the subject: "As for the prophet who prophesies peace, when the word of that prophet comes to pass, then it will be known that the Lord has truly sent the prophet" (28 9; cf. I Sam 3 19 and I Kings 8 56).

The difficulty of applying this criterion is easily discernible, for it can be effectively used only in retrospect. But even then the standard has little value when one recognizes (1) the general nature of many prophetic words, (2) the conditional aspect of prophecy, and (3) the fact that this criterion deals only with the narrowly predictive words of prophecy[36]. Furthermore, the biblical record differs as to the nature of the message to which this word must be applied. Jeremiah wishes to limit this criterion of fulfillment to the evaluation of the prophecies of weal (28 9), whereas the book of Deuteronomy would extend it to include predictions of woe (18 21-22)[37].

The prophetic oracles are predominantly general; that is, they speak in vague terms of war, pestilence, famine, the peril from the North, the sword, and so forth. Besides this, they are constantly subjected to a process of actualization whereby a word for a previous generation is turned into a message of the living present[38]. This means, then, that a prophetic word may find any number of "fulfillments",

---

[36] Jacob, Quelques remarques sur les faux prophètes, 479; Tilson, False Prophets in the Old Testament, 177—181; and Osswald, Falsche Prophetie im Alten Testament, 23—26.

[37] Osswald, Falsche Prophetie im Alten Testament, 24, is certainly correct in this regard.

[38] N. W. Porteous, Actualization and the Prophetic Criticism of the Cult, in: Tradition und Situation, 93—105; and P. R. Ackroyd, The Vitality of the Word of God in the Old Testament: A Contribution to the Study of the Transmission of O. T. Material, Annual of the Swedish Theological Institute 1 (1962), 7—23. A classic example of the re-interpretation of a prophetic word is Nathan's promise to David in II Sam 7. See L. Rost's model of tradition-historical analysis, Die Überlieferung von der Thronnachfolge Davids, 1926, reprinted in: Das Kleine Credo und andere Studien zum Alten Testament, 1965, 119—253.

each of which is in many respects different from what was spoken of in the original prophecy.

The conditional element of prophecy also militates against the successful employment of the criterion of non-fulfillment to a prophetic message. The prophet Jonah is the most glaring example here; were the criterion of non-fulfillment applied in this instance this pitiful figure would become even more deserving of sympathy. And what of the unfulfilled prophecies of the great prophets? Is one to conclude that Jeremiah and Isaiah are false prophets because some of their predictions failed to materialize[39]? That would be stooping to one level of the popular mind in ancient Israel, as seen in quotations by Isaiah, Jeremiah and Ezekiel. The former refers to those who say: "Let him make haste, let him speed his work that we might see it; let the purpose of the Holy One of Israel draw near, and let it come, that we may know it!" (Isa 5 19). Likewise Jeremiah's listeners say to him: "Where is the word of the Lord? Let it come!" (17 15) and Ezekiel mentions a proverb to this effect: "The days grow long, and every

[39] For the problem of unfulfilled prophetic predictions, see the literature cited in Lindblom, Prophecy in Ancient Israel, 199 note 149, and A. Kuenen, The Prophets and Prophecy in Israel, 1877 (reprinted in 1969), 98—275, who has collected a list of prophetic predictions that did not materialize. Some of the more glaring unfulfilled prophetic words of Isaiah and Jeremiah are the Zion oracles of Isaiah, the predictions that Damascus would become a heap of ruins (Isa 17 1f.), that Israel and Syria would be despoiled before the child named Maher-shalal-hash-baz knows how to cry "My father" or "My mother" (Isa 8 4), that Judah and Israel would reunite (Jer 3 15ff.), that Hophra of Egypt would be given into the hand of his enemies (Jer 44 30), that Judah would return to Palestine after seventy years (Jer 29 10). Numerous unfulfilled predictions occur in other prophetic books, for example Ezek 4 6 5 2. 12 17 20 26—28 29 8ff. 21 40—48 Hag 2 1-9. 19-23 Zech 4 1-14 6 9-15; etc. Mention may also be made of Huldah's promise that Josiah would be gathered to his fathers in peace (II Kings 22 18-20), particularly since she was the one to judge the divine revelation of the law book discovered in Josiah's era. However, the most noticeable failure of prophetic promise is II Isaiah, for this poetic masterpiece is permeated with unfulfilled predictions (Cyrus did not worship Yahweh; Babylon was not destroyed; the desert did not blossom like a garden, etc.). In this regard Kuhl, The Prophets of Israel, 1960, 144, has observed that "were Deutero-Isaiah to be measured by the yardstick of a Jeremiah he would surely rate very low by reason of his salvation utterances," yet Deutero-Isaiah differs from salvation prophets, for he represents "neither chauvinism nor syncophancy, but comfort and uplift for the despairing, dejected and broken in heart". In view of the abundance of unfulfilled prophetic words within the oracles of genuine prophets of Yahweh, E. Osswald's remark that "their faith was erring faith" (Falsche Prophetie im Alten Testament, 26; cf. also Hempel, Vom irrenden Glauben) is quite to the point. Despite the failure of every prophetic word to find fulfillment in history, the apocalypticists used earlier prophecy as the criterion for calculations as to the course of sacred history (Fohrer, Introduction to the Old Testament, 483).

vision comes to nought" (13 22). Does not the response of the people determine God's action toward them[40]?

But the most devastating criticism of the use of the standard of nonfulfillment arises from the fact that it is limited to the narrowly predictive prophetic words. While it is true that Old Testament scholarship went too far in denying the predictive element of prophecy, a trend that is being recognized and corrected in various quarters today[41], it nonetheless is a fact that prediction in the narrow sense occupies a minor role in ancient prophecy. As a consequence any valid criterion of true prophecy would have to apply to the total prophetic word and not to a peripheral element.

### Promise of Weal or Woe

A second criterion is the promise of weal or woe. It has become almost a commonplace that the great prophets predicted doom, whereas the false prophets promised peace to the people of God. Hence it is no surprise that more recent writers have emphasized the cultic function of prophecy, namely the promotion of the welfare of the state. This correction of a false understanding, however, must not lead one to reject the criterion of the prediction of weal without careful consideration, even if a message of salvation is based on the dual ideas of election and theocracy.

The prophet Jeremiah is said to have judged the comforting promise of Hananiah on the basis of the prophetic tradition: "The prophets who preceded you and me from ancient times prophesied war, famine, and pestilence against many countries and great kingdoms" (28 8). Such a verdict would seem to be confirmed by the message of the opponents of Micaiah ben Imlah (I Kings 22), for here one sees the contrasting words of weal and woe, and only the judgmental word is confirmed by subsequent events as truthful. Further confirmation of the view that false prophets declared peace may be found in Ezekiel's tirade against these deluded prophets: "Because, yea, because they have misled my people, saying, 'Peace', when there is no peace, and because, when the people build a wall, these prophets daub it with whitewash; ..." (13 10).

---

[40] Fohrer, Action of God and Decision of Man in the Old Testament, in: Biblical Essays, 1966, 31—39; and Scott, The Relevance of the Prophets, 9—12, have discussed man's role in determining whether predicted judgment or grace are actualized.

[41] H. H. Rowley, The Nature of Old Testament Prophecy in the Light of Recent Study, 131; and R. Dunkerly, Prophecy and Prediction, ExposT 61 (1949—50), 260—263. The ability of Yahweh to foresee and predict historical events before their actual occurrence is particularly significant to II Isaiah. It is ironical that the grandiose predictions by this author failed to materialize at all.

But the prophetic word of these false messages was not fixed, as can be gathered from a closer look at the words of Deuteronomy and Micah. The assurance that the people of God need not be afraid of the prophets who speak a word that does not come to pass (Dtn 18 22) would be meaningless unless the prophecy were one of woe. Even more certain is the allusion in Mic 3 5b, where the prophet charges his opponents with changing their message according to the reward proffered but they "declare war against him who puts nothing into their mouths".

This criterion is further complicated by the fact that the preserved prophecies of true prophets contain words of weal and woe almost side by side. This is especially true of Isaiah (7 1ff.), where the Zion theology cannot be attributed to a later hand[42]. In a real sense one must admit that the Deuteronomic promises and the theology of Hananiah are in a straight line with the Isaianic tradition. Perhaps, however, there is a very significant difference on the part of Hananiah, for he does not appear to link the promises to the demand for faith as in Isaiah or the fulfillment of the Mosaic ethical demands as in Deuteronomy[43].

By way of contrast, the false prophets promise weal to those who deserve a word of judgment: "They say continually to those who despise the word of the Lord, 'It shall be well with you'; and to every one who stubbornly follows his own heart, they say, 'No evil shall come upon you'" (Jer 23 17). Small wonder that the people took comfort in such phrases as "the temple of the Lord" and "With us is God, no evil shall befall us". Such confidence in the holy city is encouraged by the prophets: "Then I said, 'Ah, Lord God, behold the prophets say to them, "You shall not see the sword, nor shall you have famine, but I will give you assured peace in this place'"" (Jer 14 13). A corollary to this is the prediction of doom to fall upon the enemies of Israel. Is one, then, to place Nahum among the false prophets, and what of the oracles against foreign nations in Amos, Jeremiah, Ezekiel and Isaiah?

Despite all of these objections to the criterion of the prediction of woe, nevertheless, there is a real sense in which the standard can be used profitably in evaluating classical prophecy, as E. Osswald has persuasively argued[44]. But the criterion can only be used with reservations, and in no sense applies to post-exilic prophecy, which stands

---

[42] Childs, Isaiah and the Assyrian Crisis, passim.

[43] For the relationship between covenant and law, see the recent discussion by W. Eichrodt, Covenant and Law, Interpr 20 (1966), 302—321; Zimmerli, The Law and the Prophets, 31—45; D. J. McCarthy, Treaty and Covenant, 1963, and E. Gerstenberger, Covenant and Commandment, JBL 84 (1965), 38—51.

[44] Falsche Prophetie im Alten Testament 18—23.

under a different "hour" in God's mysterious dealings with the people Israel[45].

## Revelatory Form

A third criterion found within the Old Testament is the manner in which revelation was received. Three facets of this standard are evident: (1) the presence or absence of ecstasy; (2) the revelation by means of a dream; and (3) the emphasis upon word or spirit.

That the true prophets experienced an ecstasy of concentration (in contrast to that of absorption) seems certain, so that one cannot deny ecstatic behavior to genuine prophecy. In fact, there seems to be no clear-cut distinction along these lines between true and false prophet. This does not imply that one is to ignore the evidence of abnormal behavior on the part of opponents of Elijah or the early bands of prophets, but rather that this ecstatic behavior, perhaps more natural to the Baal cult, was an early stage through which Israelite prophecy passed (cf. Num 11 10ff.).

A clearer word can be said about the revelation by dreams[46]. According to Jeremiah, a prophet who receives the message through dreams is by that very fact a false prophet. This viewpoint comes out most sharply in 23 25-28, which consists of a caustic attack upon those whose motto is "I have dreamed, I have dreamed!" and concludes with an exhortation followed by a question: "Let the prophet who has a dream tell the dream, but let him who has my word speak my word faithfully. What has straw in common with wheat? says the Lord."

Nevertheless, dreams were not always looked upon with disfavor in the Old Testament (Gen 28 10ff. Joel 2 28 [3 1] Num 12 6 I Sam 28 6). In fact, the dream was especially important as a revelatory form in the wisdom and apocalyptic literature. Moreover, the prophetic literature abounds in visions, so that this appeal to the presence of dreams loses much of its force when one perceives the kinship of vision and dream[47].

---

[45] E. Osswald's words are quite compelling: "The true prophet must be able to distinguish whether a historical hour stands under the wrath or the love of God" (Falsche Prophetie im Alten Testament 22). This shift in the historical situation (between Isaiah and Hananiah, in this instance) has been emphasized most forcefully by M. Buber, Falsche Propheten, 278—280.

[46] W. Zimmerli, Das Wort und die Träume, Der Grundriß, Schweizerische Reformations-Monatsschrift (1939), 197—203; E. L. Ehrlich, Der Traum im Alten Testament, 1953; I. Mendelsohn, Dream, IDB I, 868f.; A. Caquot, Les songes et leur interprétation, 1959; A. Resch, Der Traum im Heilsplan Gottes, 1959, and J. A. Sanford, Dreams, God's Forgotten Language, 1968.

[47] Lindblom, Prophecy in Ancient Israel, 125, notes that there is a "close affinity between an ecstatic vision and a dream". If true, this would complicate matters

Again it has been argued that true prophets were transmitters of the Word of God, whereas the false prophets emphasized the Spirit[48]. Unfortunately, such a distinction between Spirit and Word can only be maintained by violence to the Hebrew text at crucial junctures (Mic 3 8, for example); perhaps it is more correct to recognize geographical interests here, Ephraim emphasizing the word of God[49].

### Allegiance to Yahweh or Baal

In the fourth place, false prophecy has been distinguished from true on the basis of undivided allegiance to Yahweh as opposed to Baal. This criterion is advanced in Dtn 13 1-3, where it is stated that even if a prophet performs a wonder but encourages apostasy to other gods he is not to be heeded, for the Lord is only testing Israel. The necessity for such a standard is illustrated by Jer 2 8. 26. 27 23 13 32 32-35 where it is said that prophets speak for Baal. Evidently this does not mean that these prophets belonged to the Baal cult, as did Elijah's opponents on Mount Carmel, but that they spoke in the name of Baal having assumed the mask of Yahweh[50]. Where the prophets belong to the Baal cult, however, the criterion under discussion would certainly apply, and there would be no difficulty in recognizing their falsity. Nevertheless, the inadequacy of this criterion in most cases is evident, for the "false prophets" served Baal while believing themselves to be devotees of Yahweh. Their error was one of ignorance, a failure to distinguish between the two gods. Of course some prophets may have been guilty of hypocrisy in this regard, but it is impossible to determine the extent of such pretense. Finally, the extra-Yahwistic

even further, for visions are central to the great prophetic books. In fact, von Rad is probably correct that the call narratives, which are chiefly visions, are intended to justify the prophetic message (Old Testament Theology, II 55). Lindblom even ventures to suggest that Jeremiah's concern over being proved wrong prompted the vision of the almond rod (*šaqed*) symbolic of Yahweh's watching over (*šoqed*) his word to fulfil it (Prophecy in Ancient Israel 139).

[48] S. Mowinckel, La connaissance de Dieu chez les Prophètes de l'Ancient Testament, RHPR 22 (1942), 80—81, writes that "c'est dans la possession de la parole que réside la différence décisive entre le vrai prophète et le prophète menteur." Mowinckel also thinks that the consciousness of divine call is the distinctive sign of a true prophet (76—77). For the contrast between spirit and word, see his article The "Spirit" and the "Word" in the Pre-Exilic Reforming Prophets.

[49] Von Rad, Old Testament Theology, II 57 note 11, appeals to Hos 9 7 for support of this view.

[50] E. Sachsse, Die Propheten des Alten Testament und ihre Gegner, 1919, 3ff. 13ff. If a prophet advocates apostasy to Baal, however, he is by that very fact no longer a genuine prophet of Yahweh.

problem is only a small part of the phenomenon of false prophecy, so that this criterion of allegiance to Yahweh or Baal cannot be used in most situations even if generally valid for some incidents[51].

### *2. Criteria Focusing upon the Man*

In brief, the criteria focusing upon the prophetic message are of relative merit, being impossible of application or impractical. But what of those centering upon the prophet himself? These have to do with the institutional nature of prophecy (the "office"), the immoral conduct of false prophets, and the conviction of having been sent.

#### Prophetic Office

First, the office of the false prophet. It has been argued that the false prophet was a professional cultic official living off the proceeds of his ministry. The existence of such cultic prophets can no longer be doubted, but the evidence in no way points to these prophets as false. While it may be true that the free charismatic prophet was more faithful to the Word of Yahweh, there is no reason to deny that exceptional cultic prophets achieved the same degree of freedom to declare the word of the Lord.

The appeal to I Kings 22 at this point is useless, for the narrative makes abundantly clear the fact that the royal prophets acted in good faith, that they gave the word which the Lord had committed to them. Nor is Amos' reply to Amaziah decisive here, for it is not at all certain that his anger is stirred over a charge of preaching for the money. Furthermore, the fact that one prophet, be he as important as Amos, scorns institutionalism does not mean that this criterion may be applied to all prophets in every period of history.

#### Immoral Conduct

The moral criterion has the sanction of Jesus of Nazareth (Mt 7 16) and has been advocated in a number of variable forms. But it was not original with Jesus; on the contrary, the prophet Jeremiah often appealed to this criterion in rejecting the words of his opponents, and Micah links this standard with institutional prophecy (3 11). The charges of adultery and lying appear together in one oracle of Jeremiah (23 14), and drunkenness is added by Isaiah (28 7).

---

[51] See the illuminating discussion of the relationship of Israelite prophets to those outside Israel by H. W. Wolff, Hauptprobleme alttestamentlicher Prophetie, 206—231, especially 207—213, where it is said that the form and conduct are old, the content new.

However, there are instances dealing with so-called false prophets where these questionable acts are absent (the opponents of Micaiah ben Imlah; Hananiah), so that this standard is not capable of use in all cases. Furthermore, it ignores the fact that even the true prophets were on occasion guilty of what must be considered immoral behavior. The most striking example is the marriage of Hosea to a prostitute, an incident that has prompted more scholarly attempts at explanation than almost any other in the Old Testament[52]. Numerous hypotheses have been put forward, none of which has been completely satisfactory, although the trend now seems to be to treat the marriage as a symbolic action revealing little if anything about the prophet's domestic situation[53].

The allegorical interpretation suffers from the absence of a symbolic meaning for the name Gomer and the presence of minute details about the weaning of the second child and the ransom price[54]. Nevertheless, the incident was allegorized in chapter two, where Gomer represents Israel and Hosea, God. Some have wished to see reference to two different women in the account, the woman of chapter three being a common prostitute, and the purity of Gomer being affirmed by viewing "a woman of harlotries" (*'ešæt zᵉnûnîm*) in 1 2 as a religious designation without physical connotations[55]. Perhaps the most often advanced view is that Gomer was a good woman at marriage and subsequently proved false to her husband, the description of the divine commission being retrospective[56]. It should be noted that this view fails to preserve God's honor, for from the ethical standpoint it would be more just for God to inform Hosea what kind of wife he was getting, rather than keeping the knowledge from him. Others have viewed Gomer as a cultic prostitute, explaining the price paid for her as payment for loss of revenue to the sanctuary at which she provided her

---

[52] For a recent re-examination of the basic interpretations of Hosea's marriage, see I. H. Eybers, The Matrimonial Life of Hosea, in: Studies on the Books of Hosea and Amos, 1964—1965, 11—34 (with extensive bibliography). The similar study by H. H. Rowley, The Marriage of Hosea, BJRL 39 (1956—57), 200—233, reprinted in: Men of God, 1963, 66—97, is still quite valuable.

[53] Von Rad, Old Testament Theology, II 138; and J. M. Ward, Hosea: A Theological Commentary, 1966, 58.

[54] The visionary interpretation, closely akin to the allegorical, participates in most of the latter's faults, while providing little that is positive. Accordingly it has few advocates.

[55] R. H. Pfeiffer, Introduction to the Old Testament, 1941, 566—573.

[56] This is in essence the conclusion of I. H. Eybers in the essay: The Matrimonial Life of Hosea. The use of *'ešæt zᵉnûnîm* instead of *zônā*, the usual word for harlot, is taken by many as indicative of a *propensity toward* evil ways. In this view, Gomer was potentially a harlot when Hosea married her.

services[57]. However, the use of *'ešæt zenûnîm* instead of *qedešā* (cultic prostitute) makes this view difficult to accept.

The most natural interpretation is to see Gomer as a common harlot, and to view the entire episode as the prophet's obedience to divine command. The marriage was intended as a symbolic action, its purpose to depict the relationship between Israel and God as one that began as a marriage between the holy God and sinful nation but was dishonored by Israel, who must be isolated and forbidden "sexual union", hence destroyed[58]. This means that the message of Hosea was not the result of a tragic domestic experience, nor does the analogy of love move from what man is like to a conclusion as to the nature of God, a basic weakness of the view that stresses the formative influence of the marriage upon the message of Hosea[59].

However one understands the marriage of Hosea, he must wrestle with the fact that it is offensive to one's moral sensitivity. Even those who interpret "woman of harlotry" as a religious designation cannot avoid this problem[60], for Hosea makes it abundantly clear that physical adultery accompanied religious apostasy to Canaanite religion. The simple fact remains that Hosea married a harlot, and that he felt certain that God commanded him to do so.

It may also be noted that the prophet Isaiah had sexual relations with "the prophetess" (*hănnebî'ā,* Isa 8 3), although it is usually assumed that she was his wife. Such an interpretation is in no way demanded by the text, however, this being an unusual way of addressing one's wife. Furthermore, why would the prophet need reliable witnesses if he merely went in to his wife? If the prophetess were not his wife, the desire for witnesses becomes understandable, since this is a dramatic symbolic action. Isaiah is also said to have wandered around Judah

---

[57] T. H. Robinson (and F. Horst), Die Zwölf Kleinen Propheten, 1954, 17; von Rad, Old Testament Theology, II 141, and others. The absence of evidence for sacred prostitution at Ugarit raises serious doubts about this view, despite the practice in Mesopotamian religion.

[58] J. Wellhausen rightly recognized that *wegăm 'ænî 'elayik* must be completed by *lo' 'abô'* (and I shall not come to you!); see Die Kleinen Propheten, 1963, 105 (unchanged reprint of 1898 edition). Prophetic symbolism is described most ably by Fohrer, Die symbolischen Handlungen der Propheten, 1953; and Die Gattung der Berichte über symbolische Handlungen der Propheten, ZAW 64 (1952), 101—120, also in: Studien zur alttestamentlichen Prophetie, 92—112. See also H. Wh. Robinson, Prophetic Symbolism, in: Old Testament Essays, edited by T. H. Robinson, 1927, 1—17; and M. P. Matheney, Jr., Interpretation of Hebrew Prophetic Symbolic Act, Enc 29 (1968), 256—263.

[59] Here I agree substantially with the conclusion of Rowley in: The Marriage of Hosea 94—97.

[60] Pfeiffer, Introduction to the Old Testament, 568.

almost naked, conduct that was quite offensive to the eighth century Israelite (20 2).

The prophet Jeremiah was guilty of what must be described as "immoral" conduct, even if to save his life or in response to a life of "martyrdom". In Jer 38 14-28 it is recorded that king Zedekiah asked the imprisoned prophet for advice but urged Jeremiah to tell a lie if asked the content of his counsel, and that the prophet answered his interrogators according to the words given him by the king. In the Confessions, Jeremiah complains bitterly about those who persecute him, praying that they be brought to destruction (17 18), their children be delivered up to famine and sword, their wives be childless and widowed, and their men and youths slain (18 21).

In actual fact, deceit appears elsewhere as a factor in early prophetic literature. Micaiah ben Imlah used deceit so often that the king had to rebuke him by saying, "How many times shall I adjure you that you speak to me nothing but the truth in the name of the Lord?" (I Kings 22 16). Similarly, Elisha advised Hazael to tell Ben-hadad, the king of Assyria, that he would recover from an illness, although assuring Hazael that the Lord had shown him that Ben-hadad would surely die (II Kings 8 7-15). Hazael obeyed the prophet, slew the king the next day, and reigned in his place[61]. The prophet Elisha is also said to have cursed some children from Bethel for mocking him, and it is reported that two she-bears promptly killed forty-two of them (II Kings 2 23 f.).

Another example of an "immoral" prophet, one who is expediently silent, is recorded in II Chr 25 14-16, where a prophet is said to have been sent to rebuke Amaziah for resorting to gods of other peoples, but stops when the king asks why he should be put to death, even if getting in the last word.

In this context it may be observed that Jeremiah's accusation that false prophets steal oracles overlooks the obvious dependence of his own message upon Micah, Isaiah's upon Amos, and Ezekiel's upon Hosea[62]. Furthermore, the passages common to Isaiah and Micah, as well as Jeremiah and Obadiah, imply borrowing from one another, or from an unknown source[63].

---

[61] Those prophets who participated in political revolutions (for example, Elisha's role in Jehu's overthrow of the ruler) must bear part of the responsibility for the terrible blood purge accompanying the *coup d'état*.

[62] For discussion of Isaiah's indebtedness to Amos, see R. Fey, Amos und Jesaja, 1963. Fey's conclusions have recently been contested by Whedbee, Isaiah and Wisdom, Chapter III.

[63] Compare Isa 2 2-4 and Mic 4 1-4; Ob 1-9 and Jer 49 7-22; Joel 4 16 Jer 25 30 Am 1 2; Mic 1 10-15 and Isa 10 27b-32; Mic 2 1-3 and Isa 5 8-10.

Although the moral criterion must be rejected, it is admitted that "false prophets" often failed to live up to the higher morality of an Amos, Isaiah or Ezekiel. The most serious charge against these false prophets was their conspiracy of silence, a failure to speak out against wrong (Hos 4 5)[64].

### Conviction of Having Been Sent

Others have called attention to the conviction that Yahweh has sent the prophet as a mark of true prophecy (Am 7 10ff. Mic 3 8)[65]. This claim, however, did not go unchallenged (Jer 23 21. 32 43 2-3), and the opponents of the great prophets felt called to their task (Jer 28 2) but were also challenged at this point (Jer 28 15). In actual fact, this conviction of having been called is outside the area of historical investigation, so that the inadequacy of such a criterion is readily seen. No one can say whether or not a prophet has stood in the council of God, even though Jeremiah thought himself capable of doing so (23 18. 21-22).

## *3. The Chronological Criterion*

By way of summary, neither the criteria centering upon the message nor those focusing upon the man are satisfactory in distinguishing true from false prophecy. But there is one other criterion that deserves discussion, since it has been applied to the prophets in Judaism (and in Islam, where Muhammed is the last prophet). This standard is chronological; it derives from the limitation of inspiration to the time from Moses to Ezra. In short, any prophet who does not belong to this period is automatically marked out as a false prophet[66]. Nonetheless, an eschatological age was envisioned when true prophecy would recommence (Joel 3 1 f. I Macc 14 41). But this standard is of no value in solving the problem of false prophecy in the Old Testament.

---

[64] D. E. Stevenson, The False Prophet, 1965, 43, uses the felicitous phrase "the lethal bludgeon of silence" in describing today's false prophets in the pulpits. Kraus, Prophetie in der Krisis, 1964, 113—115, also emphasizes the failure of the false prophets to tell Israel of her guilt.

[65] S. H. Blank, Of a Truth the Lord Hath Sent Me: An Inquiry into the Source of the Prophet's Authority. Clements, Prophecy and Covenant, 38, admits that most prophets began their activity after a special call, and distinguishes Amos from these other messengers by the intensity of his conviction of having been sent, but such a decision is nothing more than a value judgment, there being no way to evaluate the intensity of the conviction of any prophet.

[66] This view was not the only one in Judaism, as seen in the Qumran community and in the writings of Josephus. See W. Foerster, From the Exile to Christ, 1964, 4—5, and below, Excursus A on False Prophecy in the New Testament Period.

What can be said, then about the various criteria discussed above? All are inadequate as a means of illuminating false prophecy, since the latter is no unified phenomenon. Consequently its solution must be sought from case to case, no single criterion nor any group of criteria fitting every instance[67]. Does this mean that the attempt to distinguish true from false prophecy in ancient Israel must be abandoned? In effect, this is the position to which one is forced, as G. Quell has argued so cogently[68]. But one can go further than Quell was willing to do; it cannot even be claimed that another prophet can in every instance distinguish the true from the false[69].

---

[67] E. Osswald, Falsche Prophetie im Alten Testament, 29.

[68] Wahre und falsche Propheten: Versuch einer Interpretation.

[69] Against Quell ibid. 206 and Jacob, Quelques remarques sur les faux prophètes, 486. However, even Quell admits that Jeremiah did not at first know whether he was a true spokesman for Yahweh and Hananiah false (46).

CHAPTER IV

# The Inevitability of False Prophecy

## A. THE TRANSITION FROM TRUE TO FALSE PROPHECY: HUMAN CULPABILITY

Since no single criterion serves to distinguish in every instance the true from the false prophet, a degree of fluidity between the two is inevitable. This fact has been perceived most clearly by K. Harms, and provides the stance from which K. Barth views I Kings 13. It is, furthermore, the implicit assumption of other biblical passages, for the Israelite prophets recognized human responsibility for conduct unbecoming to a messenger of Yahweh.

### *1. The Biblical Testimony*

#### Prophetic Legend

Of primary significance in this regard is the prophetic legend in I Kings 13. Here the man of God from Judah, who is certainly depicted as a true prophet, becomes false to his commission and must hear Yahweh's judgment upon him from the lips of one who is a "false prophet", but who at this moment at least has been transformed into a genuine spokesman for Yahweh. The change in each is almost beyond his knowledge or volition, the man of God having disobeyed in ignorance — and in a kind of naïveté, a simple faith in the truthfulness of others in the profession of prophecy — and the old prophet from Bethel speaking a word of doom without having sought it or without desiring it, and apparently wishing it could be reversed.

The Balaam narrative also tells of a prophet who set out to pronounce a curse upon Israel, but who encountered the angelic representative of Yahweh on the way and subsequently uttered only words of weal for the people of God. This favorable message is announced despite the threat posed by the king who had summoned him to curse Israel or the reward promised him if he but say the right words. Balaam's response to Balak soars to lofty heights: "Must I not take heed to speak what the Lord puts in my mouth?", a sentiment highly reminiscent of Micaiah's answer to the messenger who sought to influence his message (I Kings 22 14). In view of Balaam's words in the present text it is difficult to understand the tradition surrounding this prophet in later times, all of which is negative and hostile except Mic 6 5. In Dtn 23 4-5 (Heb 5-6) and in II Pet 2 15 Balaam is accused of having a desire for base gain, despite the fact that he refused to alter his message so as to receive lavish gifts. Balaam is also infamous for having instigated Baal worship (Num 25 1-3 31 16 Rev 2 14); accordingly, it is claimed that he was put to death by the Israelites because he led Israel astray so that a plague broke out upon the people (Josh 13 22 Num 31 8. 16). Regardless of the explanation for this hostile attitude to Balaam, which must rest upon an association of this prophet with the apostasy at Peor, the fact remains that Balaam is said to have set out with one message in mind and to have uttered still another after the experience with a threatening angel[1].

Still another prophetic legend belongs to this discussion, namely the story of Elijah at Mount Carmel and its sequel (I Kings 18—19). Here this dauntless defender of Yahwism stands up for his God despite almost insurmountable odds, only to flee like any coward upon learning of Jezebel's intentions. The story does not hesitate to depict Elijah as a defeated hero of bygone days, one who was wasting away in self-pity and who was recognized as dispensable by the One whom he had defended so courageously in a stronger moment. While it may be amiss to view Elijah as a false prophet in this episode, it certainly is true that such behavior moves in the direction of proving false to God, and stands under the divine correction[2]. Such is the import of the majestic theophany in which the "still small voice" comes to the prophet after the elaborate fanfare of mighty wind, earthquake and fire[3], communicating to Elijah the promise that the zeal of this defender of Yahweh was not in vain, but would be rewarded by the survival of seven thousand in Israel who will neither bow the knee to Baal nor kiss the god's image, but at the same time commanding Elijah to anoint *a successor*.

---

[1] O. Eißfeldt, The Old Testament, an Introduction, 189 note 6, gives an extensive bibliography on the Balaam narrative.

[2] For a helpful treatment with exhaustive bibliography, see H. H. Rowley, Elijah on Mount Carmel, BJRL 43 (1960—61), 190—219, reprinted in: Men of God, 37—65. Two other studies deserve mention, namely G. Fohrer's Elia, 1957, and J. J. Stamm's Elia am Horeb, in: Studia Biblica et Semitica, Th. C. Vriezen Festschrift, 1966, 327—334.

[3] J. Jeremias, Theophanie, 1965, 110—112, recognizes the strange note in I Kings 19, indeed the polemical tone. Von Rad, Old Testament Theology, II 19f., argues against the attempt to see a polemic in this text, but his view is not altogether satisfactory. J. K. Kuntz, The Self-Revelation of God, 1967, 147—154, recognizes a contrast between the theophany to Moses (Ex 33 12-23) and the prophetic boldness described on that occasion, and this divine self-revelation to submissive Elijah. Kuntz views the word as an attack against cultic over-confidence.

## Prophetic Fiction

This transition within a prophet is illustrated most vividly in prophetic fiction. Jonah is depicted as a true prophet who has been given a word for the Ninevites, but who refuses to proclaim it because of a desire to see them go into ruin unwarned. This prophet to whom Yahweh had spoken directly becomes a runaway, and behaves with less human compassion than the pagan sailors on whose ship he is traveling; but God disciplines his prophet, knocking him to his knees in submission. This rebellious prophet, smarting from the chastening blows of the God who had commissioned him, sets out at last on the original mission, announcing the word of judgment in almost brutal fashion ("Yet forty days, and Nineveh shall be overthrown!" 3 4). Despite the absence of any conditional element to the prophecy, the people *and animals* repent in the hope that God will have mercy upon them. When their hope is vindicated, the prophet of Yahweh wallows in self-pity, complaining that he knew that Yahweh's real nature is to forgive, so that Jonah has now been discredited among these people. The story closes with an illustration of Yahweh's gentle treatment of erring and angry prophets[4].

## Prophetic Oracles

The possibility of transition from true prophecy to false is assumed in a well known passage from Jeremiah's complaints (15 19). Having been accused of seducing the prophet, Yahweh warns Jeremiah that "if you return, I will restore you, and you shall stand before me; if you utter what is precious, and not what is worthless, you shall be as my mouth; they shall turn to you, but you shall not turn to them." Implicit in the warning is the possibility that Jeremiah could choose to utter words other than what Yahweh has spoken[5]. In other words, his status as prophet is dependent upon obedience to the divine word. The fact that one has once been a prophet of Yahweh does not guarantee continued service as his spokesman, just as election by God did not mean that Israel could not be cast off and trodden under foot of man (cf. Am 3 2 Isa 5 1ff.).

In brief, the fluidity between true and false prophecy is a factor to be reckoned with in the older prophetic legends of Balaam, Elijah

---

[4] Of recent studies, three deserve mention here: E. Bickerman, Les deux erreurs du Prophète Jonas, RHPR 45 (1965), 232—264; P. L. Trible, Studies in the Book of Jonah, unpublished Ph. D. Dissertation, Columbia, 1964; and H. W. Wolff, Studien zum Jonabuch, 1965.

[5] Von Rad, Old Testament Theology, II 202, rightly observes that this passage portrays Jeremiah as having betrayed Yahweh.

and the man of God from Judah, in prophetic fiction and in later prophetic oracles. If it is possible for a true prophet to become false and for a false prophet to speak an authentic word, there must be some basic reasons for this shift, some temptations that appeared especially alluring to prophets.

## 2. *Reasons for the Change*

### Desire for Success

It will be argued below that the total impact of the prophetic witness was minimal. When one takes into consideration the criterion of fulfillment as validation of authenticity as a spokesman of Yahweh, the problem is immediately apparent. From this perspective the *desire for success* is not simply a selfish attitude of one who wishes to see his message confirmed in history, rather it is an authentic expression of hope that God's word is trustworthy[6]. If the truth or falsity of a prophet's vocation depended upon the fulfillment or non-fulfillment of his predictions, then success became a seal of divine approbation, and no longer a mere happy coincidence. This desire for success, then, must have prompted many prophets to speak messages that contributed to the possibility of their succeeding with the populace. Such a wish becomes almost a motto for Ezekiel: "Then you shall know that a prophet has been in your midst." Again, the desire for success would appear to be a theme of the enigmatic story of Jonah, even if this motif be subsidiary to the attack upon the error residing in the narrow nationalism of the Ezra-Nehemiah reforms. This exclusivism, perhaps necessary to the survival of Judaism in the Persian period and afterwards, provided the context in which the prophet had to go against almost impossible odds when proclaiming a universalistic message, or even when announcing a word of judgment upon Judah. Small wonder the attack upon the position represented by Ezra and Nehemiah came indirectly, that is, through fiction (Jonah and Ruth). Few were the prophets who could distinguish patriotism from the divine will, for election theology contributed immeasurably to the conviction that the Jews alone were the chosen of God[7].

[6] Jacob, Quelques remarques sur les faux prophètes, 484—486, calls attention to four obstacles to true prophecy: (1) kingship; (2) tradition; (3) the crowd; and (4) the desire for success. His contribution to the following discussion is readily apparent to the knowledgeable reader.

[7] The understanding of the elect one over against the rest of mankind reflected in Gen 12 1-3 and Isa 49 6 was too easily forgotten, particularly when the nations oppressed the chosen of Yahweh. Intense nationalism is a natural result, and the dialogue within the post-exilic community is particularly illuminating. The presence

The task of a prophet was a difficult one, made all the more unbearable because of the apparent failure that was the lot of most prophets. While Jeremiah was able to find some comfort in voicing his anguished emotions, others may have found the fire within their bones less grievous than the alternative of speaking for a God who seemed unworthy of their service. But even Jeremiah never transcended his situation sufficiently to interpret his suffering redemptively, even if recognizing that the prophetic office implied "martyrdom"[8]. Accordingly, complaint comes to be the dominant feeling in Jeremiah's oracles, and in the Confessions "there is not one single instance of hope, no occasion when he gives thanks to Jahweh for granting him redemptive insight or for allowing him some success. What a difference from the defiant boasting of Micah!"[9]

The prophet who discerned the divine purpose in prophetic martyrdom was Deutero-Isaiah, who emphasizes the redemptive nature of the sufferings of the Servant of the Lord. It is not the Servant's renown that is emphasized, "but his wretchedness and the contempt in which he is held"[10]. Here the rupture between the man and the prophetic task that had arisen with Jeremiah and prompted such agonizing questions has been repaired, and the identity between office and man maintained. Suffering is now viewed as God's means of accomplishing salvation for the Gentiles. In this way the desire for success can be satisfied in the face of apparent defeat, for it is affirmed that God will "see the fruit of the travail of his soul and be satisfied" (Isa 53 11a), for many will by this means be accounted righteous.

---

of this difference of opinion is reflected not only in such works as Ezra-Nehemiah and Esther on one side, Ruth and Jonah on the other, but also in the glosses added to prophetic texts. In view of the fact that the central problem confronting the people of God was her self-understanding over against those not chosen by Yahweh, both in terms of the incorporation of non-Yahwistic literary forms and concepts into her faith, and in religious or social behavior, it would be especially helpful to study Old Testament literature in terms of the tension between nationalism and universalism.

[8] Von Rad, Old Testament Theology, II 206.

[9] Ibid. 203. Von Rad's discussion of the confessions is particularly poignant (see also Die Konfessionen Jeremias, EvTh 1936, 265—276). The view of H. Kremers, Leidensgemeinschaft mit Gott im Alten Testament, EvTh 13 (1953), 122—140, that the related Baruch document is a *via dolorosa* is rejected by Fohrer, who prefers to think in terms of an attempt to show how prophetic oracles have been fulfilled in history (Introduction to the Old Testament 399). J. Bright, The Prophetic Reminiscence: Its Place and Function in the Book of Jeremiah, in: Biblical Essays, 1966, 27ff., thinks of such passages as 1 4-19 13 1-11 18 1-12 19 1-13 24 16 1-18 27 32 6ab-15. 17-25 35, which he calls A[1], as occasioned by conflict with prophets, thus in a real sense a testimonial document to establish the validity of Jeremiah's ministry and word (29).

[10] Von Rad, Old Testament Theology, II 256.

## The King

Another obstacle to the faithful fulfillment of the prophetic task is found in *the king*, especially in Israel, but often in Judah[11]. The royal interests frequently ran contrary to the divine, and any cult sponsored by the king was expected to further the interests of its sponsor. The issue comes into clear focus in the confrontation between Amos and Amaziah at Bethel (Am 7 10-17). The two-fold message of Amos that Jeroboam would be slain and Israel exiled was viewed as conspiracy by the priest, and a report was immediately given to the king. Jeroboam's reaction was to banish Amos from his kingdom, a decision that Amaziah transmitted to the prophet with considerable insult, first in the choice of the term seer (*ḥozæ*) rather than *nabî'*, and in the implicit accusation of professionalism. Amos reacts to both with strong emotion, responding that he is a *nabî'*[12] and has been called by Yahweh from tending cattle and working as a dresser of sycamore trees, commissioned, that is, to "prophesy to my people Israel". The priest advises Amos to flee to Judah and survive, but never again to prophesy at Bethel, "for it is *the king's sanctuary*, and it is *a temple of the kingdom*" (7 13). Würthwein's thesis that Amaziah's intentions are benevolent[13] can hardly be correct in view of the hostile reaction of Amos, who tells the priest that Yahweh's word to him is one of total loss — of his wife, who will be treated as a harlot in the city by the invading army, his children, who will be slain by the sword, his land, which will be divided among conquering soldiers, and his freedom and office, for he will be taken captive and die in an unclean land[14]. The underlying assumption of king and priest is that the royal sanctuaries exist for the sole function of promoting the welfare of the state, and anyone who fails to comply with this purpose is in danger of the king's wrath.

A similar perspective is reflected in the story of Micaiah ben Imlah (I Kings 22)[15], where the prophetic function of strengthening the king

---

[11] A. S. Herbert, Worship in Ancient Israel, 1959, 41, writes that the prophetic function was to strengthen the king, and that frequent inquiry by royalty forced the prophet to rely on artificial stimulants, false prophecy being the result.

[12] H. N. Richardson, A Critical Note on Amos 7 14, JBL 85 (1966), 89, rightly understands the response in terms of the Ugaritic *lu/la emphatica*. Clements, Prophecy and Covenant, 37 note 1, gives a useful bibliography of significant discussions of this much debated question. To this list may be added H. Schmid, Nicht Prophet bin ich, noch bin ich Prophetensohn: zur Erklärung von Amos 7 14 a, Jud 23 (1967), 68—75. [13] Amos-Studien 19—24.

[14] The desire to end one's days in familiar territory, that is, one's native land, is vividly depicted in "The Story of Si-Nuhe," ANET 18—22, and in the incident recorded in II Sam 19 31-40, where the aged Barzillai declines David's invitation to come to Jerusalem to live, asking permission to remain in his own city to die.

[15] To be discussed more fully below.

in his military endeavors is at stake. Here the prophets employed at the sanctuary in Bethel are identified as possessions of the king, and the prophet who dampened the morale of the people is subject to royal action. This supportive role of prophecy is seen most clearly in the Elisha narratives, which depict this prophet as a soldier for Yahweh, and even apply to him the phrase "my father, the chariots of Israel and their teams"[16].

In view of this attitude to prophecy on the part of the kings of Israel, Hosea's hostility to the kingship assumes new dimensions. The Elijah narratives were a fresh reminder that the desires of the king were at variance with those of Yahweh's messengers, and that the prophets were in danger so long as this situation persisted. Small wonder that all Israel's troubles were thought to have begun at Gilgal (Hos 9 15), for both the memory of persecution of prophets by Ahab and the present turmoil in the royal palace were sufficient cause to call into question the divine participation in the establishment of the monarchy[17].

In Judah the Davidic and Zion traditions were complicating factors, and one discerns a curious ambivalence in the prophetic literature from the south, especially in the message of Isaiah. But even here a growing disillusionment with Davidic rulers can be discerned in the most avowedly royal eschatology, each oracle pointing backwards to the period of charismatic leadership during the tribal federation, and forward to the coming of an idealized figure who almost amounts to a *Davidus redivivus*[18].

Particularly illuminating in this context is the ministry of Jeremiah, who functions both as antagonist and protagonist to the rulers

---

[16] After von Rad, Old Testament Theology, II 29. The episode recorded in II Kings 13 14-19 describes Elisha in such terms, and has king Joash utter the expression on an occasion of the prophet's illness. The court prophets, like Elisha in this story, are described as supporters of royal policy, but also like Elisha are quite forthright in criticism of the king's conduct. This is especially true of Nathan and Gad, who assist David even when rebuking him, for in leading him to the recognition of his folly the prophets make possible the continuation of the Davidic dynasty. Another way in which prophets assisted the king was in building up and sustaining the morale of the army; this function within the context of holy war comes out most clearly in Dtn, but also in the literature from Qumran (where priests have taken over the task of morale building).

[17] The two variant traditions in Samuel as to the origin of the monarchy, one positive and the other negative, indicate that the questioning of Yahweh's role in the establishment of kingship has its roots in early times. Gottwald, All the Kingdoms of the Earth, 119—146, has discussed the historical background of Hosea most helpfully.

[18] Harrelson, Nonroyal Motifs in the Royal Eschatology, in: Israel's Prophetic Heritage 147—165.

of his day. His animosity toward Jehoiakim was especially pronounced, and the feeling was mutual (Jer 22 13-19 36); on the other hand, the weak and vacillating king Zedekiah appears to have had high regard for Jeremiah, even if unwilling to act on the basis of advice given by the prophet (38 14-28). Jeremiah's contemporary, Ezekiel, also represents a certain hesitancy to accept the monarchy as divinely commissioned, as the preference for the term *nagîd* over *mælæk* indicates.

But the situation is not quite so simple, for the existence of the monarchy was also a pre-requisite of prophecy, and the prophetic movement fell into disrepute soon after the collapse of the kingship, the one great exception being Deutero-Isaiah. This indicates that in a very real sense the kingship provided a serious obstacle to prophecy but at the same time called forth the prophetic witness in all its splendor. Of course, the Solomonic era, which is apparently devoid of prophecy, cannot be understood in these terms, possibly because of the belief that Solomon had immediate access to God, since he was considered a sage to whom Yahweh revealed his will in dreams, and the fact that no serious crisis from outside Israel arose[19]. This assumes, to be sure, that prophecy in the tenth century had not yet been democratized or received its primarily social cast typical of the great eighth century figures. That being so, the era of peace and *Aufklärung* was not conducive to the emergence of prophetic spokesmen, for their essential function at that time was to assist in military crises.

## Popular Theology

A third explanation for the shift from true to false prophecy is the *popular theology* of the worshippers to whom prophets were sent. This religion of Israel (described above as a faith characterized by confidence in God's faithfulness, satisfaction with the status quo, defiance, despair, doubt as to God's justice, and historical pragmatism) influenced the prophets both positively and negatively. Affirmatively, in that they participated in the same struggle of the soul over the disparity between the promise and actual fulfillment, felt the same confidence that evil must be punished if God be just, recognized clearly that the claims of faith were frequently at variance with the course of history in the ancient Near East, and questioned the ways of God with bitter complaint. Negatively, too, for in the borrowing of popular concepts for the purposes of communication, and in the

[19] C. Westermann, Propheten, 1500ff., rightly perceives the significance of the monarchy for an adequate understanding of Israelite prophecy. Solomon's role in wisdom has been questioned by R. B. Y. Scott, Solomon and the Beginnings of Wisdom in Israel, in: Wisdom in Israel and in the Ancient Near East 262—279.

course of *argumentum ad hominem*, some prophets were swayed by the religion of the masses, and became subject to it rather than to the word of God[20].

This popular religion was a syncretistic one, having incorporated elements of Baalism, Yahwism, and Assyro-Babylonian beliefs[21]. Canaanite cultic influence can be seen in the sacrificial system, festivals, sacral prostitution, asherim, and Cherubim, while theological impact is evident in the notion of creation (El Elyon), stress upon nature and fertility, tolerance growing out of incipient monotheism, the metaphor of Yahweh as the rider upon the clouds, and the idea of *ṣᵉbaʼôt šᵉmăyim*[22]. Assyro-Babylonian influence arose as the result of royal vassalage, especially during the reigns of Manasseh and Ahaz. This worship of idols of every kind of creeping thing and wild beast, together with the adulation of Tammuz and the sun is described most vividly by Ezekiel (8 5-18). Actually such idolatry is no radically new departure, as can be seen in the fact that a golden bull was employed in Yahwistic worship from early times (this is certainly the reason for Jeroboam's selection of this object, for it represents a desire to outarchaize David)[23], as was a bronze serpent, which Hezekiah removed from the temple during his reform of Yahwism[24]. Having practiced this sort of worship from earliest times, the Israelites who fled to Egypt naturally succumb to the temptation to devote their lives to the queen of heaven, especially since it pays to do so. Their ardor while kissing calves and zeal in performing cultic rites had made a lasting impression upon the prophets, and Egyptian bondage was to introduce nothing essentially new in this regard (cf. Hos 13 2).

---

[20] Magical elements were already present in priestly and prophetic circles, so that the further step in the direction of popular theology was a small one.

[21] Perhaps it would be more correct to follow Y. Kaufmann, The Religion of Israel, 138—147, where it is maintained that Israel's religion was not genuine syncretism, since other gods were not thought of as equal to Yahweh.

[22] N. C. Habel, Yahweh versus Baal, 1964; A. S. Kapelrud, The Ras Shamra Discoveries and the Old Testament, 1965; E. Jacob, Ras Shamra-Ugarit et l'Ancien Testament, 1960; G. Östborn, Yahweh and Baal, 1956; J. Gray, The Legacy of Canaan, 1965; S. Segert, Survival of Canaanite Elements in Israelite Religion, in: Studi sull' Oriente e la Bibbia (Festschrift für P. Giovanni Rinaldi), 1967, 155—161; W. Harrelson, Prophecy and Syncretism, AndNQ 4 (1964), 6—19; and G. W. Ahlström, Aspects of Syncretism in Israelite Religion, 1963.

[23] Harrelson, Calf, Golden, IDB I, 489. See also M. Aberbach and L. Smolar, Aaron, Jeroboam, and the Golden Calves, JBL 86 (1967), 129—140, where the striking similarities between Aaron and Jeroboam are emphasized.

[24] For a recent discussion of the bronze serpent, see K. R. Joines, The Bronze Serpent in the Israelite Cult, JBL 87 (1968), 245—256, where it is argued that the bronze serpent is of Mesopotamian and Canaanite origin, depicts the fecundizing power of Yahweh, and is unrelated to the Mosaic serpent except in popular tradition.

In most of these areas the gulf between prophecy and people was almost insurpassable, and this in itself constituted an additional barrier to communication. But the popular religion was also closely akin to that of genuine prophecy, particularly in the holy war traditions and concomitant nationalism. The living memory of initial success during the conquest, and the ever-present recollection of the greatness of the Davidic era, placed an indelible stamp upon Israelite faith, gave to it a conviction that Yahweh would be with his people to give victory over her foes. The admonition "Fear not" together with the promise "For I am with thee"[25] appear in contexts as diverse in nature as in age, testifying to the permanence of this conviction that Yahweh's fate was in some way tied up with that of Israel. Even if the great prophets were able to divorce themselves from any such association, they still found it most difficult to think in terms of a termination of the special relationship between Israel and her God.

## Power of Tradition

Still another reason for the transition from true to false prophecy was the *power of tradition*. This influence of the past assumed various forms, each with a distinct *Sitz im Leben*. The basic forms of tradition, however, are the theologies surrounding the themes of David, Sinai, the exodus, wilderness wandering and conquest, Zion, patriarchs, and the divine dwelling place (ark and temple), all of which make up the concept of an elect people[26]. Every one of these tradition complexes contributed something worthwhile to Yahwism, while at the same time constituting an ever-present danger, that of permitting the people to assume that this special relationship with God was not dependent upon Israel's response to the total purpose of God, that is, of blessing all the peoples of the earth. But even some prophets were prone to think that since the God who made these promises contained in the traditions of election was faithful, he would fulfill them despite Israel's sinful conduct. Accordingly reasons for such unconditional love were put forth, particularly the marriage symbol and the appeal to the *ḥæsæd* of Yahweh[27], the honor (reputation) of the God of Israel among the Gentiles, and the remnant, a brand plucked from burning embers.

It is within this context alone that the conflict between Jeremiah and Hananiah is to be understood, for the latter was a faithful pre-

---

[25] K. W. Neubauer, Erwägungen zu Amos 5 4-15, ZAW 78 (1966), 297—302; and H. D. Preuss, "... ich will mit dir sein!"

[26] Von Rad, Old Testament Theology, II, has discussed the various transformations of the traditions with keen insight.

[27] N. Glueck, Ḥesed in the Bible, 1967, originally published in German in 1927.

server of the ancient traditions so precious to Isaiah of Jerusalem (Jer 28). Hananiah speaks an oracle *to Jeremiah* in the presence of priests and people declaring God's intention to break the yoke of the king of Babylon, returning to Jerusalem both the temple vessels (stolen by Nebuchadrezzar) and the exiles. Jeremiah's response is "Amen! May the Lord do so"; however, prophets who preceded us from ancient times "prophesied war, famine, and pestilence against many countries and great kingdoms" (v. 8), and anyone who declares peace will be certified as a genuine spokesman of Yahweh when the word of weal comes to pass. Hananiah's reaction is to break the yoke-bars Jeremiah wears at Yahweh's command, and to declare that Nebuchadrezzar's power over other peoples will be broken in two years. To this message Jeremiah has no response, and goes his way; however, at a later time the Lord gives him a retort for Hananiah: "You have broken wooden bars, but I will make in their place bars of iron" (v. 13), for Nebuchadrezzar has been given sovereignty over all peoples and beasts, and as for you, because you have made this people trust in a lie, God will remove you from the earth. The story ends with the report of Hananiah's death in that same year.

Quell's warning that biblical scholars stand in danger of a too negative approach to Hananiah and too positive one to Jeremiah is well taken[28], for the narrative leaves no doubt that Hananiah proclaims his word under the conviction that its source is divine. Moreover, he makes use of the prophetic oracular formula and *propheticum perfectum* (28 2. 11), and is so certain of the truth of his prediction that he dares to set a time limit to it (two years as over against the three generations suggested by Jeremiah)[29]. The absence of "to me" in the oracular formula in no way affects this claim of genuineness, and there is absolutely no basis for the view that Hananiah was an insincere, lying prophet or that he belonged to the immoral prophets elsewhere condemned by Jeremiah[30]. On the contrary, Kraus is right that "thus we confront in Hananiah a prophetic exponent of a salvation theology of Israel grounded in election and covenant"[31].

Jeremiah's initial response to Hananiah's prophecy reveals that he too has been nurtured in the election faith and retains human wishes for Israel despite the prophetic office that has demanded the sublimation of these feelings. W. Rudolph's comment in this regard is classic: "In him is the same patriotism, the same love of his enslaved people; what more would he want than that the promise of well-being

---

[28] Wahre und falsche Propheten: Versuch einer Interpretation 60ff.

[29] W. Rudolph, Jeremia, 1958, 163.

[30] Ibid. and emphasized by Kraus, Prophetie in der Krisis, 90f.

[31] Prophetie in der Krisis 91.

be fulfilled!"[32] At the same time, however, Rudolph recognizes that Jeremiah has been disciplined by his calling to transcend such human wishes[33]. The criterion invoked by Jeremiah that previous prophets had proclaimed judgment must not be employed as a standard for literary criticism, for it is problematical, indeed, a half truth[34]. In reality, even the message of Jeremiah does not fit into such a Procrustean bed; the fact is that most prophets of woe envisioned a time of salvation after the judgment had fallen. Furthermore, Quell is correct that in this instance Jeremiah does not know whether he is an authentic spokesman of Yahweh or not; consequently, he goes on his way, not having an answer for the moment[35].

The narrative makes clear, however, that in this particular situation a message steeped in the election faith was out of place. This is the import of the delayed word that came to Jeremiah after he had been humiliated before the masses ("The prophet to the people is like a helpless lamb that is led to the slaughtering house" [Jer 11 10])"[36]. Now Jeremiah announces that Hananiah will be sent no more, except to his grave. This time there is no counter-demonstration; Jeremiah has spoken the last word[37]. The timeliness of a prophetic word has been emphasized most helpfully by Buber, who writes that "it is not whether salvation or disaster is prophesied, but whether the prophecy, whatever it is, agrees with the divine demand meant by a certain historical situation, that is important. In days of false security a shaking and stirring word of disaster is befitting, the outstretched finger pointing to the historically approaching catastrophe, the hand beating upon hardened hearts; whereas in times of great adversity, out of which liberation is liable now or again to occur, in times of regret and repentance, a strengthening and unifying word of salvation is appropriate"[38].

---

[32] Jeremia 164.

[33] Ibid.

[34] Ibid. 165, and Kraus, Prophetie in der Krisis, 95.

[35] Wahre und falsche Prophetie: Versuch einer Interpretation 45. See also Rudolph, Jeremia, 165; and Kraus, Prophetie in der Krisis, 95. Prophetic indecision also appears in the initial response of Nathan to David's announced intention to build a temple, and the very different word from God that came that night (II Sam 7).

[36] Kraus, Prophetie in der Krisis, 98.

[37] Ibid. 103. If Jeremiah's actions in wearing the yoke had been "a thorn in the eyes of the *nabî*'s" (Rudolph, Jeremia, 163), his word to Hananiah must have been a sword in the heart!

[38] The Prophetic Faith, 1949, 178. Too little attention has been given to the different audience for the prophetic word, recognized by von Rad (Old Testament Theology, II 171) as the explanation for certain features of Isaiah's message about the anointed of Yahweh. It may be that many of the contradictions within a prophetic book were

## Emergence of Individualism

A fifth reason for the change from true to false prophecy arises from the *emergence of individualism* to new and unprecedented proportions during the sixth century. Although the individual had always been important in ancient Israel, particularly in legal matters and in private devotion, the concept of group solidarity by which families, clans and nations preserved their integrity began to give way once the process of urbanization became a factor in Israel. Such a breakdown of tribal solidarity created the context in which the eighth century reforming prophets proclaimed their words of warning, and the lessening of national ties brought about by the policies of the conquering Assyro-Babylonian armies set the stage for Jeremiah and Ezekiel, both of whom wrestle with the despair of a chastened people who interpreted their situation fatalistically in terms of a proverb, "Our fathers have eaten sour grapes and the children's teeth are set on edge" (cf. Lam 5 7). This growth in the role of individualism is, furthermore, ample testimony to the emerging impact of wisdom thinking in Israel, for basic to *ḥåkmā* was the analysis of individual experience. Another aspect of this emphasis on the individual was the concern to maintain the goodness of God despite numerous exceptions to this dogma. So long as appeal could be made to family or clan, the unjust suffering of one individual posed no real problem, for one's merits might fall to a succeeding generation. However, once this solidarity with the past and future representatives of a family was forgotten, a single example of innocent suffering called into question God's goodness or power[39]. This fact alone is sufficient explanation for the frequent asseverations of the righteousness of God[40], the doxologies of judgment that have found their way into prophetic and psalmodic literature.

There is a real sense in which much so-called false prophecy was an attempt to justify the ways of God to man. To one who assumes the justice of God, a word of judgment upon all Israel means that the

---

addressed to different circles, words of woe to the sinful crowd, promise of well being to a faithful few. Buber's point, it should be noted, that a basic shift in historical circumstances demands a changed message, is most clearly seen by contrasting apocalypticism with prophecy.

[39] The surprising thing is that Yahweh's power was not questioned more often, for the history of Israel certainly provided ample opportunity for such thinking. However, the motif of punishment for sin provided a convincing explanation for any catastrophe.

[40] Von Rad, "Righteousness" and "Life" in the Cultic Language of the Psalms, in: The Problem of the Hexateuch and Other Essays 243—266 (originally in: Festschrift für A. Bertholet, 1950, 418—437), and S. B. Frost, Asseveration by Thanksgiving, VT 8 (1958), 380—390.

righteous will be punished along with the wicked. Therefore, it may be that many so-called false prophets uttered their messages out of a genuine desire to see God reward goodness, as well as a conviction that such would be the case. If one recognizes the presence, even in the most wicked generation, of a small group of faithful believers, it is easy to understand how some prophets would proclaim well-being, for the piety of the true people of God could not be in vain. Furthermore, it is likely that many of the oracles of *šalôm* were directed at this small conclave of true, obedient children of God, and were only subsequently taken to be general oracles for all Israel. The moving etiological narrative of the destruction of Sodom and Gomorrah (Gen 18) has as its main point the conviction that Yahweh acts in justice, even when destroying entire cities. The account of Abraham's intercession for the cities leaves the impression that there were not even ten righteous inhabitants, and that those who fit this category (Lot and his children) were spared. The sequel makes quite clear how far Yahweh was willing to go in evaluating the righteousness of the city dwellers, for two of the three who were delivered act in a rather shameful, (even if under the circumstances, necessary) manner to procure children. The justice of God is also affirmed in the story about Moses' intercession for a rebellious people, indeed his willingness to be excluded from the heavenly book, although here the wrath of God almost overshadows his justice (Ex 32). In the face of overwhelming evidence to the contrary, the justice of God was defended by courageous souls, some of whom may have erred in the direction of too frequent proclamation of well being, but without whose witness Israel's faith would be terribly impoverished.

Such concern for the individual as is manifested in these narratives had profound effect upon the prophetic ministries of those charged with a message for the defeated people in Judah and in Babylonia. Jeremiah witnesses to this shift in a remarkable manner, the line between word of God and prophetic word almost disappearing in his oracles[41]. Likewise Ezekiel is moved by a concern for each individual that transforms him into a sort of pastor for troubled souls[42], one whose responsibility is to warn the godless lest their blood be held against him. Moreover, this individualistic perspective contributed to the growing tendency to divide society into two groups, the righteous (*ṣăddîqîm*) and sinners (*rešaʿîm*). Such a black and white division,

---

[41] Von Rad, Old Testament Theology, II 193; see also O. Kaiser, Wort des Propheten und Wort Gottes, in: Tradition und Situation 75—92, where the word of God is said to be born out of the dialogue between tradition and the contemporary situation; and Wolff, Das Zitat im Prophetenspruch, passim.

[42] Von Rad, Old Testament Theology, II 232.

typical of Psalms and Proverbs, even appears in late prophetic eschatology, particularly in Am 9 10, where judgment is envisioned for sinners only, whereas the original message had been all-inclusive. Because of the seriousness with which the rights of the individual were taken toward the end of the monarchy, the prophetic "I" becomes much more prominent and the relationship to the "thou" more intense, since complaint is a major part of the prophetic response[43]. Just as the prophets direct their charges against God, so the people raise constant protest against them. Von Rad has observed in this regard that "the direct result of this individualization of prophecy was the increase in the number of collisions with those who saw the same situation with different eyes, and whom we call 'false prophets'"[44]. It may be added that such conflict was inevitable since the prophetic office more and more invaded the personal lives of the called of Yahweh, and even Jeremiah could describe his experience in terms of being led step by step "nearer to the terrifying night of abandonment by God"[45].

When these obstacles to true prophecy are taken into consideration, it is no great surprise that many true prophets became false to their calling. But the opposite may also be the case: the false prophet may become true to Yahweh's intention. Such is the irrefutable message contained in I Kings 13, where the professional prophet takes up against his will the word of Yahweh. But the same may be said of the opponents of Micaiah ben Imlah and of Hananiah, both of whom are true to their understanding of the divine will, are indeed true prophets while speaking an untrue message. The words of G. Quell must not be allowed to fall to the ground: "Who is to tell us, then, that false prophecy with its power of error cannot be an instrument in the hand of God?"[46] Just as in the thinking of Isaiah and Habakkuk God can use the cruel armies of Assyria, renowned for their policy of calculated frightening (cf. Nahum), to punish wayward Israel and Judah, so He can employ spokesmen against their will, can use even the most reprobate of his creatures to bring about his purposes in human affairs[47].

In this context it may not be amiss to examine the biblical view of God's response to prophets who had failed to live up to their calling,

---

[43] Ibid. 265.

[44] Ibid.

[45] Ibid. 274. This feeling of abandonment by God finds frequent echo in the Psalms.

[46] Wahre und falsche Propheten: Versuch einer Interpretation 194.

[47] The author of II Esdras recognized the problem caused by such thinking, and wrestled with the issue of further punishment to fall upon a wicked agent of Yahweh (cf. Isaiah on Assyria). The ability of God to create something out of "nothing" provides food for thought in this context, for just as chaotic matter can be transformed into the scene for the divine-human drama (Gen 1 1—2 4a), so even those opposed to God can be employed in the refinery to separate dross from pure metal.

or who found the task too demanding. The examples most pertinent to this discussion are the Elijah and Jonah narratives, in both of which Yahweh shows remarkable patience. In this regard the narratives are closer to the book of Job[48], which depicts God as one who welcomes doubting questions that border on blasphemy and who approves the accuser rather than the rigidly orthodox representatives of official religion, than to Deuteronomy (13 5) or Ezekiel (14 10), which demand the death sentence for the offender. Still another prophetic example deserves mention here, namely the experience of Jeremiah who resolved to withhold the word of God until he found that it was an inner fire that could not be contained, and who was told that things would not get any easier and that increased resolve and courage would be required if he wished to remain Yahweh's spokesman.

If man's conduct and speech ultimately contribute to the divine purpose, whether this is their intention or not, then one is forced to recognize that the problem of false prophecy transcends the human situation, indeed that divine sovereignty may provide an explanation for the presence of men with equal conviction of having been sent by Yahweh despite contradictory messages. This means that the dark side of God, the "demonic"[49], must be taken into consideration, for the ultimate source of false prophecy is God himself!

## B. FALSE PROPHECY AS GOD'S MEANS OF TESTING ISRAEL: DIVINE RESPONSIBILITY

### *1. The "Demonic" in Yahweh*[50]

The human factor is only half of the explanation for false prophecy, for whatever part man may have played in delivering a message that had no origin external to the spokesman, or in interpreting it in a manner alien to the intention, was dwarfed by the divine responsibility for this phenomenon. Biblical literature abounds in this sentiment, irrespective of the age of composition. The belief that everything, good or bad[51], came from Yahweh provides the rationale for this view, and demands that the element of the demonic be considered.

[48] The function of the divine theophany as the resolution of the problem confronting Job must not be overlooked. Here one finds a majestic rebuke of anthropocentricity, a poignant reminder of the mystery of God.

[49] The "shadow side" of God has been described most penetratingly by C. G. Jung, Answer to Job, 1954; and by P. Volz, Das Dämonische in Jahwe, 1924.

[50] For lack of a better word, the adjective "demonic" is used here, and quotation marks will be dispensed with. The context should make quite clear, however, that the term refers to an aspect of God's redemptive action.

[51] Isa 45 6f. Dtn 32 39.

From the beginning it was recognized that there was something unfathomable and sinister about Yahweh[52]; an element of the unpredictable was present in every encounter. This dark side of Yahweh may be seen in numerous incidents within the Old Testament, each showing a different facet of the demonic. While R. S. Kluger may be partially correct in her contention that "in the Old Testament, God himself, through his dark side, works on man as 'the power that always wills the bad, and always creates the good'"[53], at least the biblical witness would generally agree that the demonic elements are under control and employed for redemptive purposes. W. Eichrodt's observation that "God's sovereign freedom to punish sin with sin if he wishes, and in that way to bring it to judgment, is quite another matter from the immoral practices of the Babylonian and Greek gods, who made false revelations to men in order to deceive them to their ruin"[54] is thus a necessary corrective to Kluger's view, even if the narratives about Micaiah son of Imlah, Saul, David and Moses (I Kings 22 19-23 16 14 19 9-10 II Sam 24 1-17 Ex 4 24) and similar passages put Yahweh in closer relationship with the pagan gods than Eichrodt admits. To the biblical writer, man was in a real sense like clay in the hands of the potter, and the dual nature of this craftsman comes out most vividly in Isa 45 7 ("I form light and create darkness, I make weal and create woe, I am the Lord, who do all these things"), Dtn 32 39 ("See now that I, even I, am he, and there is no god beside me; I kill and I make alive; I wound and I heal; and there is none that can deliver out of my hand") and I Sam 2 6 ("The Lord kills and brings to life; he brings down to Sheol and raises up").

This sinister side of Yahweh appears in the account of the fall of man in Gen 3, the serpent having been created by God, in a sense making the Creator responsible for temptation and rendering the verdict "Behold, it was very good" something of a shallow mockery. Similarly, the Jacob narrative contains an account of the demonic attack upon the fleeing Jacob (Gen 32 24-30), although this incident has been marvelously transformed to serve as a conversion experience of unprecedented import[55]. In the Moses narrative there is a story about Yahweh's attack upon Moses at an inn, during which the life

[52] H. Ringgren, Israelite Religion, 1966, 73. Even the revelation of the divine name is enshrouded in mystery (*'æhyǣ 'ašær 'æhyǣ*, Ex 3 14), for God refuses to be slave to man. Nowhere does this appear more poignantly than in the book of Job. The idea of the holy may provide the basis for this mystery; see R. Otto, The Idea of the Holy, 1958, passim, where attention is called to the *mysterium tremendum et fascinans*.

[53] Satan in the Old Testament, 1967, 113.

[54] Theology of the Old Testament, II 1967, 426 note 5.

[55] For a stimulating discussion in this vein see W. Harrelson, Interpreting the Old Testament, 1964, 63.

of this leader was preserved by the quick thinking of Zipporah, who circumcised her son and touched Yahweh at the appropriate spot (Ex 4 24-26)[56]. Demonic behavior is also said to have assisted Moses in his confrontation with the Pharaoh, or at least to have hardened the heart of the ruler so as to heighten the miraculous element of the exodus (Ex 9 12 10 1). This latter motif is present also in Dtn 2 30, where Yahweh is thought to have hardened the heart of Sihon the king of Heshbon so that he might fall into the hands of the Israelites, and in Josh 11 20, which asserts that this principle was operative for all of the inhabitants of Canaan, Yahweh hardening their hearts to lead them to battle against the mighty Israelites.

### Historical Literature

The kings of Israel were also subject to the demonic action of Yahweh. In Judg 9 23 it is reported that God sent an evil spirit between Abimelech and the men of Shechem, while I Sam 16 14 and 19 9-10 tell of Yahweh's action in destroying the first king of Israel because of his refusal to obey Samuel and his presumption in performing priestly rites. But perhaps the most notable incident of the demonic is found in II Sam 24 1-17, which the Chronicler changed radically by introducing the figure of Satan. Here Yahweh prompts David to take a census, then becomes angry when the king obeys, sending the prophet Gad to announce Yahweh's intention to punish Israel and to give David a choice of three years of famine, three months of fleeing before enemies, or three days of pestilence. The harshness of this passage is somewhat mitigated by the report that Yahweh repented of the evil and stayed his hand before Jerusalem itself was smitten. Again, in I Kings 12 15 God moves Rehoboam to reject the request of the people, in order to bring about a rupture in the kingdom.

### Prophetic Literature

Not only is the demonic a factor in historical literature, but it also appears in prophetic and wisdom literature. In Am 3 6b the question is asked, "Does evil befall a city unless the Lord has done it?"; this belongs to a series of questions the answer of which is an emphatic "no"[57]. Even more poignant is the claim of Isa 29 10 that

---

[56] H. Kosmala, The "Bloody Husband", VT 12 (1962), 14—28, gives a helpful treatment of this difficult passage, and provides useful bibliography. For more recent discussion, see P. Middlekoop, The Significance of the Story of the Bloody Husband, Ex 4 24-26, SEAJTh 8 (1967), 34—38.

[57] Much has recently been made of Amos' use of rhetorical questions as proof of wisdom influence, although the argument is far from persuasive. See my article, The Influence of the Wise upon Amos 46f.

"the Lord has poured out upon you a spirit of deep sleep, and has closed your eyes, the prophets, and covered your heads, the seers", and the complaint of Isa 63 17 ("O Lord, why dost thou make me err from thy ways and harden our heart, so that we fear thee not?"). The prophet Jeremiah felt himself to be a victim of Yahweh's deceit (15 18b "Wilt thou be to me like a deceitful brook, like waters that fail?" and 20 7 "O Lord, thou hast deceived me, and I was deceived[58]; thou art stronger than I, and thou hast prevailed. I have become a laughing-stock all the day; everyone mocks me"). However, the crucial passages in prophetic literature are Am 4 6-12 Isa 6 9-13 Ezek 14 1-11 20 25 f., to be discussed below in some detail.

## Wisdom Literature

A basic presupposition of wisdom literature is the freedom of God to act regardless of man's conduct, much being made of the disparity between man's intentions and God's actual deeds[59]. But the demonic element is also present, especially in the prologue of Job. Here the accuser is an official of Yahweh, and succeeds in manipulating God sufficiently to make Job's lot miserable indeed. Furthermore, even human wisdom is not free from the demonic, as can be seen most clearly in the story of Yahweh's making void the sage counsel of Ahithophel (II Sam 17 14)[60]. Small wonder Qoheleth has lost all faith in life's meaning, for it has become apparent to him that neither God nor nature smiles upon man, who is no better off than the animals. Qoheleth knows that the experience of Job is explainable only in terms of divine caprice[61], the playful amusement of a God who uses man for

[58] Heschel, The Prophets, 113, translates "O Lord, Thou hast seduced me, and I am seduced; Thou hast raped me And I am overcome."

[59] Amenemope 19:16 reads: "One thing are the words which men say, Another is that which the god does" (ANET 423), to which may be compared Prov 19 21 20 24 21 30ff. This has been treated by K. Sethe, Der Mensch denkt, Gott lenkt, bei den alten Ägyptern, Nachrichten von der Gesellschaft der Wissenschaften zu Göttingen, 1925, 141ff.; and H. Gese, Lehre und Wirklichkeit in der alten Weisheit, 1958, 29—50.

[60] A surprising negative attitude to wisdom in the Old Testament has been perceived by H. Cazelles, Les débuts de la Sagesse en Israël, in: Les Sagesses du Proche-Orient ancien, 1963, 34—36.

[61] This fact has been emphasized by C. G. Jung, Answer to Job. The mysterious freedom of the unknowable One (Job 28) is understood in terms of a God who answers Job's charges of unfair treatment by a display of power, and only subsequent reflection on God's part, under the seductive charms of Sophia, lead him to make known to man another side of his Being. The cross is this divine declaration of compassion, the answer to Job. However, the dark side of God is still evident behind the prayer of Jesus requesting that the Father not lead into temptation and in the theology reflected in the Apocalypse of John. In this understanding of God Jung has moved a long way from the positions of the author of Job, or Qoheleth even.

target practice and who pays no heed to cries of the downtrodden — at least, until his own good time (Job 6 4 24 1-12). Moreover, the certainty of death stands as a constant reminder of nature's cruel treatment of mankind, so that Qoheleth justifiably denies any meaning to life. The pathos of his cry, "'Vanity of vanities, all is vanity', saith Qoheleth", arises from the fact that the only genuine source of meaning, God, has failed Qoheleth[62]. In a very real sense, the recognition of the demonic in Yahweh has led to the rejection of the goodness of God, has resulted in a desire to avoid God's attention!

### 2. *Exegesis of Biblical Passages*

#### Amos 4 6-12

Am 4 6-12 has been recognized as a reversal of the cultic recitation of *Heilsgeschichte*[63]; here it is claimed that nature itself is under Yahweh's control and is wielded as an effective means of discipline, nay punishment. The passage is a unit held together by the refrain, "Yet you did not return unto me" and by the thought sequence. In fact, it is possible that 4 4-5 also belongs to the unit, as Sellin suggested[64], for this would imply that the passage begins and ends with a reference to the idolatrous sanctuaries of Bethel and Gilgal. The presence of the refrain, recalling Isa 9 13 Jer 15 19 Hos 7 10 Isa 5 25 9 12. 17. 21 10 4, indicates that prophets may have composed oracles in a series of strophes even when not patterning their message after ritual procedure as in Am 1 6—2 8, although the hand of a redactor cannot be ruled out[65]. Seven chastisements are mentioned (famine[66], drought, blight and mildew, locust[67], pestilence[68], battle and earthquake), their se-

[62] The fundamental religious stance of Qoheleth has been emphasized by H. Gese, Die Krisis der Weisheit bei Koheleth, in: Les Sagesses du Proche-Orient ancien 139—151; and R. Gordis, Koheleth — The Man and His World, 1968, originally in 1951.

[63] A. Weiser, Das Buch der zwölf Kleinen Propheten, 1949, 154; von Rad, Old Testament Theology, I 181; and R. Smend, Das Nein des Amos, 412.

[64] Das Zwölfprophetenbuch übersetzt und erklärt, I 1922, 221. This assumes that the original conclusion of the passage has been removed and the doxology inserted in its place.

[65] J. P. Hyatt, Amos, in: Peake's Commentary on the Bible, 1962, 621.

[66] In contrast to the famine of Am 8 11-14, which is all the more horrible from the theological standpoint.

[67] As is well known, the prophet Joel developed this theme to eschatological proportions. For literature, see Fohrer, Introduction to the Old Testament, 425f.

[68] In view of the meanings attached to the Ugaritic root *drkt* it is tempting to translate this text "I sent among you a pestilence like the authority/rule of Egypt." This is certainly the case in 8 14, which should read "As the sovereign of Beersheba lives . . ."

quence being dramatic rather than chronological[69]. The reference is to past events, and language is chosen so as to emphasize repeated incidents. An element of irony occurs both in the phraseology ("For so you love to do" and "*proclaim* freewill offerings, *publish* them") and in the reversal of the content of the recitation of *ṣidqôt* Yahweh.

It has been suggested that the key to the passage is 4 12c ("Prepare to meet your God, O Israel"), which calls Israel to get ready for a covenant renewal similar to the original covenant between God and Israel in Ex 19[70]. However, a more likely interpretation is the view that this passage belongs to the language of holy war and implies a theophany for judgment, Israel being warned to get ready for the appearance of a punishing Judge whose patience has run out[71]. In this way the absence of a specified punishment is understandable, it being an unnamed threat left intentionally vague as was customary in oaths[72]. Accordingly, the doxology of judgment added to this unit recognizes the justice of God despite the punishment that had fallen upon the exiles and praises Yahweh of hosts for his creative, redemptive and judgmental qualities. Not without justification has A. Weiser written: "The confrontation with the God of the catastrophes is radically different. As an opponent God now stands over against the people who go on their way unmindful of him"[73].

This passage alone is sufficient warning against a one-sided emphasis upon history as the scene of Yahweh's actions. The claim that the distinctive feature of Yahwistic faith is the belief that God acted in history rather than in nature must not overlook the fact that nature is also under Yahweh's sovereignty. Furthermore, it is becoming increasingly clear that the gods of other peoples of the ancient Near East were thought to have controlled the course of history (compare the Mesha Inscription), so that the claim of uniqueness at this point must not be pressed. The excessive stress upon the historical as the scene of divine action, whatever apologetic value it may possess, nevertheless ignores the basic witness of a large segment of the Old Testament, namely wisdom literature, which moves within the realm of creation faith[74].

---

as Jacob, Ras Shamra-Ugarit et l'Ancien Testament, 65f., correctly renders it. On tish root see M. Dahood, Ugaritic *DRKT* and Biblical *DEREK*, ThSt 15 (1954), 626—631.

[69] Sellin, Das Zwölfprophetenbuch übersetzt und erklärt, 220—221.

[70] W. Brueggemann, Amos IV 4-13 and Israel's Covenant Worship, VT 15 (1965), 1—15.

[71] See the author's Amos and the Theophanic Tradition 204. 208.

[72] R. S. Cripps, A Critical and Exegetical Commentary on the Book of Amos, 1955, 175; and W. R. Harper, Amos and Hosea, 1905, 103.

[73] Das Buch der zwölf Kleinen Propheten 156.

[74] G. Fohrer, Prophetie und Geschichte, in: Studien zur alttestamentlichen Prophetie 265—293, especially 270 (originally published in ThLZ 89, 1964, 481—500); B.

## I Kings 22 1-40

The divine responsibility for false prophecy is nowhere expressed more unequivocally than in the story of Micaiah ben Imlah (I Kings 22 1-40). Desirous of taking Ramoth-gilead from the Syrians, Ahab enlists his vassal Jehoshaphat, but agrees to consult prophets for a word from the Lord before embarking on the effort, a custom throughout the ancient Near East (cf. Zakir of Hamath). The message of these prophets, approximately four hundred in number, is positive: "Go up; for the Lord will give it into the hand of the king" (v. 6). Not content with such unanimity, Jehoshaphat asks if there is another prophet of the Lord of whom inquiry may be made, and is told about Micaiah son of Imlah, a man whose "evil" messages concerning Ahab had failed to endear him to the king. Nevertheless, Micaiah is summoned, and as the kings sit in their royal robes at the gate of Samaria the prophets prophesy, one of them taking horns of iron and asserting that with these the Israelites would destroy the Syrians (cf. Dtn 33 17). Having been urged by the messenger summoning him to speak favorably to the king, and having answered that he could speak only what the Lord says to him, Micaiah faces Ahab and advises him to go up and triumph. However, the king recognizes the irony in these words so out of character ("How many times shall I adjure you that you speak to me nothing but the truth in the name of the Lord"? v. 16), and is then told the real word of God: Micaiah had seen all Israel scattered upon the mountains as sheep without a shepherd. Ahab's response is in the nature of "I told you so" to Jehoshaphat, and Micaiah continues to describe the vision: The Lord, sitting upon a throne beside the host of heaven, asked who would entice Ahab to his destruction, and was answered by a spirit who agreed to be a lying spirit in the mouth of *all his* prophets. Within this greater drama between Micaiah and the king there takes place another, the confrontation between Zedekiah and Micaiah. This earlier wielder of horns of iron smites Micaiah on the cheek, asking how the spirit left him to speak to Micaiah, and hears words of horror in return. Whereupon Ahab orders the arrest and imprisonment of Micaiah, and commands that he be fed scant fare of bread and water until the king's return in peace. Micaiah cannot resist the retort that if the king returns in peace, the Lord has not spoken by him. But Ahab's fate has been sealed, and despite efforts to disguise

---

Albrektson, History and the Gods, 1967; and W. Zimmerli, Ort und Grenze der Weisheit im Rahmen der alttestamentlichen Theologie, in: Les Sagesses du Proche-Orient ancien 121—137. The valuable study by Albrektson deserves a further word, for it gives a thorough analysis of the literature of the ancient Near East, showing that the idea of God's acting in and controlling history does not distinguish Israel from her neighbors, but is a *point of kinship*!

himself in battle and to divert the death angel to Jehoshaphat, a stray arrow is guided by Yahweh to an unprotected area of Ahab's chest. So the king dies.

The importance of this story cannot be overstated; besides its significance in the clarification of false prophecy, this narrative reveals an early tendency toward monotheism (Yahweh as king surrounded by the host of heaven), points to the strict monistic perspective of early Yahwism, and attributes prophecy in general to a supernatural origin[75]. But the recognition that Yahweh is responsible for lying prophecy sets the phenomenon of false prophecy in a new light. There can be no question about the fact that this story depicts the "false prophets" as men who gave in good faith the message conveyed to them, and portrays God as the source of this lie, even if mediated by a spirit.

This story is quite straightforward, but demands comment at a number of points. The integrity of its hero warns against a too-sharp distinction between pre-classical and classical prophecy, for Micaiah approaches the heights of Amos or Isaiah. Indeed, the kinship of the vision with that of Isaiah's call is striking[76]. Moreover, the narrative suggests that such courageous conduct is normal for Micaiah, it having stamped itself indelibly in the memory of Ahab ("But I hate him, for he never prophesies good concerning me, but evil" and "How many times shall I adjure you ... ?"). The story also indicates that the kings of Israel and Judah approach prophecy from different assumptions; for Ahab the function of the prophet is to serve the goals of the state, so that the four hundred can even be called "his prophets" (v. 22), whereas Jehoshaphat thinks of the prophet as one whose task is to communicate the divine word[77]. The irony is that the agents of the state are transformed into instruments of God without their knowledge or volition. This is accomplished by an evil spirit, which is in essence the spirit of prophecy, unless H. Ringgren is correct that behind this story lies the notion of an evil spirit or demon (*harûaḥ*)[78]. Finally, it may be asked why Ahab does not summon Elijah, who was active during this time, and over against whom a comparable story places four hundred and fifty opponents at Mount Carmel. Perhaps the answer rests somewhere between the thesis that Elijah's real name was Micaiah, the

[75] S. Szikszai, Micaiah, IDB II, 372.

[76] H. Wildberger, Jesaja, 1968, 235.

[77] J. Gray, I and II Kings, 399. The messenger has accepted the perspective of his master, and attempts to persuade Micaiah to go along with the crowd so that the morale of the army will be invincible. Pedersen, Israel, I—II 143, thinks of the messenger's purpose as influencing the will of the prophet so as to cause him actually to *see* victory.

[78] Israelite Religion 94.

name "Yahweh is my God" being chosen to symbolize his total impact upon a Baalized worship[79], and the view that Elijah was not summoned because of a reputation for contrary advice even more pronounced than that of Micaiah, one that would endanger the morale of the people[80]. This may indeed be as insoluble a mystery as Josiah's inquiry from the prophetess Huldah as to the authenticity of the word of God in the newly discovered book of the law, a choice all the more puzzling because of the slight of Jeremiah[81].

## Isaiah 6 9-12

The call narrative of Isaiah deserves mention in this context, since it describes the divine commission to this prophet in terms of making the heart of the people fat, their ears heavy and shutting their eyes lest they see, hear and understand, and turn for healing (cf. 63 17). Isaiah rightly objects to this kind of function with the question, "How long, O Lord?" and is told that he is to prophesy in this manner "until cities lie waste without inhabitant, and houses without men, and the land is utterly desolate" (6 9-11).

The failure of the Israelite to distinguish between cause and effect softens the harshness of this commission somewhat for modern critics, but the fact remains that Isaiah felt compelled to describe his call with such language and without apology. Behind the description rests the knowledge that clarity and insistence of the word of God increase unbelief and rebellion, just as constant noise dulls one's sensitivity[82]. But von Rad has rightly seen that there is more to this idea of hardening of hearts than a general law of the psychology of religion[83]. Nor is the interpretation of this concept as an intellectual difficulty (F. Hesse) acceptable to von Rad, who correctly emphasizes the hardening of Israel as "a particular mode of Yahweh's historical dealings with her", and points to the beginning, not the end, of his work[84]. The prophet

---

[79] Gray, I and II Kings, 400. R. Halevi, Micaiah ben Imlah, the Ideal Prophet (Modern Hebrew) Bet Miqra' 12 (1966—67), 102—106, links this account with the Balaam narrative and I Kings 13 as illustrative of the Deuteronomist's view of the ideal prophetic type (Dtn 18 15-22).

[80] Gray, I and II Kings, 400.

[81] Unless those who think of Jeremiah's ministry as beginning considerably later than the reform are correct. For this view see J. P. Hyatt, The Beginning of Jeremiah's Ministry, ZAW 78 (1966), 204—214; and C. F. Whitley, Carchemish and Jeremiah, ibid. 80 (1968), 38—49.

[82] R. B. Y. Scott, Isaiah, in: IB V, 212.

[83] Old Testament Theology II 151f.

[84] Ibid. 155.

perceives that the utter destruction of the people of God will not mean the end of Yahweh, and is under no illusion as to the result of his activity[85].

## Ezekiel 14 1-11

Ezek 14 1-11 makes the point that false prophecy is caused not just by self-delusion and the influence of idolatrous clients, but also by the divine will itself[86]. Two distinct sections appear, the first (1-5) describing the divine response to inquiry of his will through the prophet by elders who have compromised their faith. Apparently these men are worshippers of Yahweh, otherwise they would not have bothered to ask about his will; but they are also devotees of the gods of Babylonia, having been persuaded that Yahweh has been shown powerless and seeing no reason to serve him exclusively[87]. This partial loyalty cannot be tolerated by the Jealous One, who announces that he will answer these idolaters immediately rather than through a prophet (so the Targum). The second unit (6-11) reads like a midrash on the first, and is characterized by a prolix style. It begins with an appeal to the idolater that he return to Yahweh, and repeats the warning that any idolater who inquires of Yahweh's word through a prophet will be answered by the Lord himself. But here is an additional note, the explanation of this divine answer: God will cut him off from his people and make him a sign and byword. There follows the customary divine threat in Ezekiel that by this means "you shall know that I am the Lord" (v. 8). The conclusion is a judgment upon prophet and inquirer alike; it is said that if a prophet speaks a word and is deceived, Yahweh has deceived him and will destroy the divine spokesman from the midst of Israel.

W. Zimmerli has attempted to explain this passage as a prophetic radicalizing of sacral law[88]. The element of truth in his contention is the strong kinship in language with the Holiness Code ("any man", "set my face against" and "cut him off from the midst of the people", "make him a sign", Lev 17 3. 8. 10. 15)[89]. This author emphasizes the

---

[85] K. Marti, Das Buch Jesaja, 1900, 67. For this entire passage see also J. A. Diaz, La ceguera del pueblo en Is 6 9-10 en relación con la acción de Dios, EstudEcles 34 (1960), 733—739.

[86] G. A. Cooke, The Book of Ezekiel, 1936, 151. F. Hesse, Das Verstockungsproblem im Alten Testament, 1955, 70, considers this passage an exception to Ezekiel's view, but this is unlikely.

[87] G. Fohrer, Ezechiel, 1955, 76.

[88] Die Eigenart der prophetischen Rede des Ezechiel, ZAW 66 (1954), 1—26 (reprinted in: Gottes Offenbarung, Gesammelte Aufsätze 148—177).

[89] Fohrer, Ezechiel, 76. Equally persuasive is the understanding of the phrase *yissā ʿawôn* as a legal term (Gottes Offenbarung, Gesammelte Aufsätze 158—161).

partial character of the knowledge in Ezek 14 1-11, wishing to see it within the larger context of God's redemptive plan for Israel. Accordingly he writes that "God will slay in order to save" and observes that "the section 14 1-11 shows men a half-truth; they have experienced the divine judgment"[90]. Zimmerli thinks of Mic 6 6-8 as the much needed corrective to the behavior of these idolaters[91].

Regardless of whether we follow Zimmerli in this approach to Ezek 14 1-11 or deny that the prophet has radicalized sacral law (Fohrer), the fact remains that Ezekiel represents Yahweh as deceiving his prophets and destroying them for speaking in their own integrity. Equally striking is this prophet's claim in 20 25 f. that Yahweh gave Israel "statutes that were not good and ordinances by which they could not have life" and "defiled them through their very gifts in making them offer by fire all their first-born" in order to horrify them and convince them that Yahweh is Lord. This remarkable passage, unique in the Old Testament in that it calls into question the holy character of the law, represents the same kind of thinking as that in 14 1-11, which G. A. Cooke has called heroic because of the willingness that man be damned for the glory of God[92], but which may more accurately be described as half-truth, and a dangerous one at that. Fortunately, God is usually thought of in nobler terms than this in the Old Testament.

Since Ezek 14 12-23 may belong to this unit and certainly echoes Am 4 6-12, it may be helpful to examine this interesting passage. Here it is said that when God smites the sinful land with his four sore acts of judgment (famine, wild beasts, sword and pestilence) even such ancient worthies as Noah, Daniel and Job if present would "deliver but their own lives by their righteousness"[93]. However, it is to be observed that if there should be any survivors to lead out sons and daughters they will serve as a means of consolation, testifying by their presence and actions that God's punishment of the people was not without cause. Set within this broader context, the harsh words of 14 9-10 lose some of their sting.

---

[90] Zimmerli, Ezechiel, 1965, 313.

[91] Ibid.

[92] The Book of Ezekiel, 219 (cf. Am 5 25 and Jer 2 2f., where sacrifice is reckoned as a *human* institution).

[93] S. Spiegel, Noah, Danel and Job, in: Ginzberg Jubilee Volume, I 1954, 205—255. The relationship of the Daniel of this passage and the hero of Ugaritic literature is uncertain, but the identity of the two is likely. For a vivid description of Yahweh in the role of an avenger, see Isa 63 1-6 (to which compare the description of Anat in ANET 136), and A. S. Kapelrud, The Violent Goddess, 1969, 19.

### *3. Theological Observations*

Three observations are in order about the theological significance of such thinking. First, it is necessary to understand the emphasis upon the demonic in Yahweh as the price Israel paid for having rejected dualism[94]. So long as a monistic orientation characterized the Israelites, Yahweh was credited with the honor or the blame for whatever happened. It is no surprise, then, to read that he is directly responsible for false prophecy. But this essentially monistic thinking had its strong points too, especially in laying the foundation for monotheism and in making demons superfluous[95]. The latter factor is not without value, and merits special attention. It is noteworthy that from the earliest stages of Israel's religion Yahweh has no consort (only later at Elephantine), and whenever he is surrounded by the heavenly hosts they are always nameless servants demanded by his status as king[96]. Accordingly, the number of demons in the Old Testament is exceedingly small (*śeʿirîm*, Lilith, *šedîm*, Azazel)[97]. Moreover, the rejection of a physical dualism made possible an openness to the created order and prevented the dangers of excessive fear of sex or idolatrous worship of it[98], so that not one reference to prophetic cultic prostitutes can be found in the Old Testament (contrast the prophetesses of Ishtar at Arbela).

Secondly, the demonic in Yahweh must be subsumed under the larger concept of divine providence; in essence deception is but a means of leading Israel to repentance or judgment, the purpose of which is salvation. Back of this notion lies the understanding of God as a father who disciplines his children because he loves them, a potter who destroys vessels that have become marred and begins anew to form more perfect specimens, a metallurgist who purges the raw ore of all impurity, a betrayed husband who isolates the beloved out of concern for her and the covenant previously established.

Finally, the demonic must be understood as God's means of testing Israel; this viewpoint is stated rather forcefully in Dtn 13 1-5. Here it is said that if a prophet gives a sign that comes true and urges the people to follow other gods than Yahweh, this man is not to be heeded, "for the Lord your God is testing you, to know whether you love the Lord your God with all your heart and with all your soul"

---

[94] Von Rad, Aspekte alttestamentlichen Weltverständnisses, EvTh 24 (1964), 57—73.

[95] Ringgren, Israelite Religion, 103.

[96] See the writer's article, *YHWH Ṣebaʾôt Šemô*: A Form-Critical Analysis, for discussion and pertinent bibliography.

[97] Ringgren, Israelite Religion, 103; and T. H. Gaster, Demon, Demonology, IDB I, 817—824.

[98] It is this attitude to human sexuality that made possible the acceptance of Song of Songs into the Hebrew canon, much to the enrichment of Judaism and Christianity.

(v. 3). Despite this attribution of the test to Yahweh, however, the unfortunate prophet is to be put to death so that the evil will be purged from their midst, a verdict that fits rather poorly with the view that Yahweh is merely testing Israel. Small wonder that Habakkuk feels it necessary to announce that the vision for which he waits will not lie (2 3a); this prophet knows too well that it could deceive! Just as God tests his people, so his prophet functions as a tester and an assayer (Jer 6 27), the purpose of which is to create a people who are responsive to the divine word. Although strong objection may be raised against the idea that God submits his creatures to tests in order to determine the constancy of their allegiance, at least the most arduously tested men in the Old Testament, Abraham and Job, emerge from the experience with deeper insights into the essential nature of God. But historical as opposed to fictional man may have found the test too much, and in the weakness of the flesh turned against everything he had previously championed. Hence the observation that genuine love does not demand proof of reciprocity may not be out of place, and the recognition in Jeremiah that the transformation of the heart of stone would come regardless of man's response is a necessary corrective to the harsher notion of the divine test (31 31-34)[99].

These observations may be set within the broader spectrum of the masterful discussion of the problem of the hardness of heart in the Old Testament by F. Hesse, who conveniently summarizes his results in six points: (1) this theme calls attention to the sovereign freedom of God who acts as he chooses without being subject to human demand; (2) but such "demonic" action is exceptional, for Yahweh has made himself known to Israel as *'anokî YHWH 'ᵆlohæka* (Ex 20 2); (3) this basic promise gives a special character to the hardening of hearts, transforming Israel's history into *Heilsgeschichte* and other people's into its opposite, views the wrath of God as a negative correlate of the promise, and interprets rebellion against the law and cult from this perspective; (4) such a threat of wrath does not negate the promise, for total rebellion makes possible a final judgment and salvation for a remnant, so that the appeal is made that life accord with the demands of the law or else the godless will be doomed; (5) *Heilsgeschichte* will come to its goal, and there will be no further rebellion, since both the depraved and enemies of God will have been destroyed, and if the promise is all embracing, then there can be no threat, for man can no longer sin (*non posse peccare*); (6) a rational dogma of retribution is thus erroneous, and man is forced to recognize the

---

[99] Fohrer, Action of God and Decision of Man in the Old Testament, in: Biblical Essays, 1966, 31—39, observes that the Old Testament is a history of decisions, not of salvation (God's act-man's decision-God's action).

mystery of God and may respond in utter faith with Deutero-Isaiah ("*Vere tu es Deus absconditus, Deus Israel salvator!*")[100].

In view of these considerations, the thesis of G. Quell that "the demonic stands in the place of truth, and the demon is God himself"[101] is true only if one with him recognizes the equally inexplicable providential mercy of the creator of heaven and earth, who is at work creating a people in whom his blessing can become manifest, transforming mankind by means of true and false prophecy[102].

---

[100] Hesse, Das Verstockungsproblem im Alten Testament, 96—98 (the passage quoted is Isa 45 15).

[101] Wahre und falsche Propheten: Versuch einer Interpretation 100.

[102] See the judicious comments by T. C. Vriezen, An Outline of Old Testament Theology, 1960, 152f. Vriezen agrees with O. Procksch that this is not really demonic, for the demonic always has something infra-personal, whereas God is "Person". Lindblom, Prophecy in Ancient Israel, 315, is in essential agreement; he writes that "Yahweh always retained, even in the thought of the prophets, an element of natural power, of 'the demonic'; but the essential element in His nature was the personal quality."

## CHAPTER V

# Israel Seeks a Solution

### A. THE PROPHETS ARE HONORED AND SILENCED

The tendency to self-willed behavior despite good counsel prompted Goethe to place the following words on the tongue of Nereus: "What! Counsel? When did ever men esteem it? Wise words in hard ears are lifeless lore. Oft as the Act may smite them when they scheme it, the people are as self-willed as before"[1]. The prophetic movement in ancient Israel experienced a similar response; its literature is replete with data pointing to the almost complete failure of the prophetic message to find root in the minds and actions of the hearers.

The history of prophecy in ancient Israel begins and ends on a low plane. The earliest narratives of prophetic activity reflect an ecstatic type of behavior, indicate that the seizure is both self-induced and contagious, and suggest professional group activity that spoke a word of well-being to the king[2]. The tension between such a portrayal of early prophecy and that reflected in later literature has been recognized by R. Rendtorff, who thinks in terms of prophets as preservers of the ancient "amphictyonic" traditions[3]. Rendtorff perceives the significance of opposing forces in the prophetic movement[4], and calls attention to the claim of later prophets to be men who stand in a long tradition, one different from that represented by Samuel, Elisha, Gad, Nathan, and Ahijah. Such historical reminiscence is evident in Jer 28 8, where previous prophets are said to have prophesied war, famine and pestilence against many countries and great kingdoms; Dtn 18 15ff., where prophets are thought of in terms of a succession to Moses; Hos 6 4 f. 9 7-9 12 14, where prophets are described as having cut down the people by their words, consequently are observed carefully and deemed

---

[1] Faust (The Meridian Library, 1950) 119.

[2] B. D. Napier, Prophets in Perspective, 1962—63, 21—24.

[3] Erwägungen zur Frühgeschichte des Prophetentums in Israel, ZThK 59 (1962), 145—167.

[4] Ibid. 152. 156. Rendtorff writes that the difference between Micaiah ben Imlah and the court prophets opposing him is not that of different forms of prophecy, since both have their roots in the "amphictyony".

fools, and where a prophet (Moses) is said to have brought Israel out of Egypt.

There are exceptional prophets, it is true, in the early narratives, but the validity of the judgment that pre-classical prophecy is on a low plane still stands. The outstanding early prophets Elijah and Micaiah ben Imlah indicate that the pre-classical prophet was not necessarily a man of low spiritual perception, and if the rebuke of David by Nathan is not pure fiction and the Elisha episode involving Naaman the Syrian has any historical authenticity, the representatives of a higher prophetic activity are more numerous, even if the total ministry of both men is on a low key[5].

Post-exilic prophecy falls under a similar judgment, its representatives being mere epigones of the great classical prophets[6]. While it is true that a later prophet like Zechariah could urge his contemporaries: "Render true judgments, show kindness and mercy each to his brother, do not oppress the widow, the fatherless, the sojourner, or the poor; and let none of you devise evil against his brother in your heart", this prophet's concern with the temple and institutional religion sets him apart from his predecessors, and identifies him more closely with his fellow prophets Haggai and the unknown author of Malachi, both of whom have similar interests, the former the rendering of decisions as to clean and unclean and the aversion of drought by restoring the temple, the latter the offering of unblemished animals in sacrifice and paying of full tithes to the Lord.

The low beginning of prophecy would not be the case, however, if Moses were viewed as a prophet, as is certainly true of Deuteronomy and perhaps Numbers. In Dtn 18 15. 18 it is promised that the Lord will raise up for Israel a prophet like Moses from among Israel, and

---

[5] Nathan is less than commendable in the last scene, where he and Bathsheba take advantage of David's advanced years to arrange for Solomon to succeed the son of Jesse. If R. de Vaux, Jerusalem and the Prophets, 1965, 6, is correct that Nathan represents a conservative trend wishing to preserve the religious tradition of the Tribal League, this selection of Solomon was particularly unwise. G. von Rad, Old Testament Theology, II 30—32, recognizes the significance of the portrait of Elisha in the narrative about Naaman the Syrian.

[6] E. Hammershaimb, Some Aspects of Old Testament Prophecy from Isaiah to Malachi, 1966, 91—112, has discussed this change in prophecy after the exile most helpfully, suggesting that the disappearance of a free society with collective guilt and punishment led to the rise of utilitarian legal concerns focused upon the individual, indeed that the structural change in society removed the prerequisites for classical prophecy. Hammershaimb considers Zechariah a faint echo of earlier prophets (107 f.) and the book of Malachi pale reminiscences of earlier prophecies of doom (109). In this regard Hammershaimb's observation that the difference between Jeremiah and Ezekiel on individualism is not to be viewed as chronological (111 f.) is well taken.

that he will be heeded, for Yahweh's words will be in his mouth and the divine wrath will await those who ignore the message. The passage in Num 12 6-8 contrasts "my servant Moses" with "a prophet", calling attention to the immediacy of the relationship between Yahweh and Moses, one in which the conversation is mouth to mouth, clearly rather than in riddles, and in mutual beholding of one another. But this understanding of Moses, although reinforced by later prophetic literature (Hos 12 13), fails to do justice to his role as law-giver and judge, and stretches the concept of prophecy rather far[7]. The same may be said of Samuel, who is certainly described in terms of prophecy, but whose contribution to Israelite society was priestly and judicial, or more correctly, that of an ancient seer in the strict sense[8].

The low point to which the prophetic movement had fallen is clear in Zech 13 2-6, and can be drawn from the fact that prophecy came to be almost defunct by Maccabean times, it being hoped that a future moment in the divine plan would restore the prophetic phenomenon to its former state. From Zechariah it can be assumed that prophecy had become so distasteful to society that it no longer is reckoned in the divine economy of salvation; it is even said that the prophet is to be put to death by his parents, and that every prophet will be ashamed of his vision and will seek to hide his identity by refusing to wear the distinctive garb of the prophet and by explaining his flesh marks, probably acquired in ecstatic prophecy, as the result of a brawl.

When one looks at the Israelite response to the prophets, this decline of prophecy to its original status becomes understandable. At no time did the prophets meet with success, save in fiction (Jonah)

[7] J. Muilenburg, The "Office" of the Prophet in Ancient Israel, 74—97, has dealt with the implications of Dtn 18 15ff., concluding that in the early traditions Moses is viewed as a mediator of the covenant and as a prophet. Von Rad, Moses, 1960, and M. Buber, Moses, 1958, give a somewhat different picture of Moses.

[8] However, there is no denying that prophetic elements appear in the description of Samuel's call and activity, as discerned by M. Newman, The Prophetic Call of Samuel, in: Israel's Prophetic Heritage 86—97; and W. F. Albright, Samuel and the Beginnings of the Prophetic Movement, 1961, the latter of whom has attempted, not very satisfactorily, it must be admitted, to solve the apparent contradictions in the description of Samuel on the basis of a fragment from Qumran that reads at I Sam 1 22 "He shall become a *nazîr* for ever," the Sefireh treaties where *nagîd* means a head of a federation, or a military commander, and the assumption that the traditions within the books of Samuel are from different periods of Samuel's life. Accordingly Albright argues that Samuel was both an Ephraimite layman and a levite; judge over all Israel and little known diviner, each in proper time and place; the conquerer of the Philistines, even though only partially; and pro-monarchic (in the sense of a *nagîd*) and against the kingship as it was established in Israel. The poem in Dtn 32 is taken as a literary monument from the time of Samuel, the first great religious reformer after Moses.

or in matters of the cult (Haggai and Zechariah). The history of prophecy is one of bitter disappointment; the prophet Hosea sums up the prophetic impact upon society in succinct fashion: "The prophet is a fool, the man of the spirit is mad, because of your great iniquity and great hatred" (9 7c. d). The possibility that Hosea here quotes his opponents only widens the gap between prophet and people. Likewise Isaiah thinks of his mission in terms of making the people incapable of seeing or hearing the divine appeal to repentance, lest they turn and be healed (6 9-10). The typical Semitic failure to distinguish between cause and effect may explain the language, but the point is certainly that the prophet, either at the occasion of his call or at the end of his ministry, conceived of his prophetic mission as one of miserable failure. The same frustration characterizes the ministry of Jeremiah, who is pictured as saying that a prophetic ministry of twenty-three years has been in vain (25 3-7). A similar response was given Ezekiel, who describes the popular pleasure at hearing his message, indeed their readiness to come to hear the word of Yahweh from him, but laments that their religion is mere lip service (33 30-33). The prophet has become to them a successful entertainer, "like one who sings love songs with a beautiful voice and plays well on an instrument", but they hear what he says and refuse to do it. These summary statements of popular response to the prophetic message are borne out in the prophetic and historical literature in marvelous fashion.

### *History of Martyrdom*

From the beginning of the Israelite nation to the end the history of prophecy is one of martyrdom[9]. The old narrative about Balaam the foreign seer shows the power of Yahweh over all magic and depicts the prophet in favorable terms; nevertheless, tradition reports his subsequent martyrdom (Num 31 8). Persecution was the order of the day during the ministry of Elijah, who himself was forced to flee for his life when threatened by the wife of Ahab. This queen's evangelistic zeal for her native religion, the Melqart worship of Tyre, is reported to have led to wholesale persecution of Yahweh prophets, one hundred of whom the steward Obadiah is reputed to have hidden and provided sustenance until Elijah could face the challenge of Baalism head-on. But even this fearless prophet who according to tradition had been unafraid to face four hundred and fifty prophets of Baal fled into the wilderness upon learning that Jezebel sought his life. Ill-treatment and

[9] Lindblom, Prophecy in Ancient Israel, 203, has rightly observed that "the history of the Israelite prophets is a history of martyrdom, the outstanding example being Jeremiah."

possibly martyrdom were also the payment given the courageous Micaiah; in any event, the prophet was struck on the cheek by another prophet, Zedekiah, and was arrested, imprisoned and placed on a fare of bread and water until Ahab returned in peace, which never happened — a stray arrow being directed by Yahweh to slay the disobedient king (I Kings 22).

The prophet Amos was told by Amaziah, the priest of Bethel, that he must flee to Judah and eat bread there (continue to live or earn his living by prophesying), for the royal sanctuary could not permit such words of woe (Am 7 10-17). As in the case of Micaiah, we are not told the fate of the prophet, for the prophetic literature was not interested in biography per se. There is mention, however, of prophets who were slain for their message. Jeremiah's life is spared after the famous "Temple Sermon" because a precedent for such a message of destruction was remembered in Micah; however, the present text reports that a precedent for slaying a prophet after such a message was also recalled, namely the incident involving a prophet named Uriah who fled to Egypt and was extradited and slain by Jehoiakim (Jer 26 20-23)[10]. Another text from Jeremiah reports that two prophets in Babylonia, Ahab and Zedekiah, whose message was one of weal, were roasted in the fire by the king of Babylon (19 21-23), even if partially justifying the execution by referring to their immoral conduct. Finally, II Chr 24 20-22 contains a tradition about a prophet named Zechariah, the son of Jehoiada the priest, who accused the people of forsaking the Lord, only to be met with conspiracy and a deadly hail of stones while in the court of the temple (cf. also Elijah's prayer in I Kings 19 14, which mentions prophets slain by the sword).

Ezekiel walked among a people whose words made him appear to be dwelling amid briers and thorns and sitting upon scorpions (2 6). But the real martyr among the prophets was Jeremiah; his suffering is given expression in poignant confessions. This prophet was considered a Quisling, a traitor to his people, and became the object of an attempt at murder on the part of his own kinsmen. Arrested for desertion during a siege of the city, Jeremiah was imprisoned, beaten, placed in a dungeon, thrown in stocks, and finally forced to accompany murderous insurrectionists to Egypt. Added to the weight of this persecution, moreover, was Jeremiah's conviction that Yahweh had seduced the prophet and was like a deceitful brook, together with the burden of enforced bachelorhood. Small wonder the Suffering Servant poems of Deutero-Isaiah have been thought to reflect the ministry of

---

[10] This pericope reads like a subsequent gloss, and perhaps should be discredited Actually Jeremiah was spared because of support by the powerful Ahikam son of Shaphan (26 24), historical precedent playing a minor role.

Jeremiah. These poems contain the apex of prophetic suffering, and, though perhaps modeled upon the life of Jeremiah, describe the fate of the author of the first three Servant poems. This unfortunate prophet is led to his death like an innocent lamb, and suffers cruel defacement and death in silence (unlike Jeremiah!).

This record of martyrdom[11] stands even if numerous unnamed prophets may have enjoyed popular favor because of a ministry and message that were unobjectionable. It is all the more impressive when one notes that ancient Israel held the prophet in awe as sacrosanct, and feared him because of the immediacy of his contact with the divine. This holy awe is surely present in the early prophetic narratives, but also rests behind later stories like those dealing with Hananiah and Pashhur (Jer 28 17 20 1-6), Amaziah (Am 7 10-17), and Pelatiah (Ezek 11 13). The harsh treatment of the prophets also forces one to re-open the question about the so-called power of the spoken word in Semitic psychology, stressed time and again by J. Pedersen[12]. It is clear that this concept did not render the spokesman immune from personal danger; however, the possibility of neutralizing a curse may explain the willingness to persecute a man of God.

In view of this history of persecution it must be asked whether the impact of prophecy upon the society of Israel was not minimal. In this regard Y. Kaufmann has written: "Yet there is abundant testimony to the small influence that the prophets exercised on their own age; it was only later that their work became a decisive factor in national life"[13]. In full agreement R. Gordis wrote: "Scorned and vilified in their own day, the prophets had now [in Qoheleth's day] attained to wide authority, and were more truly alive centuries after their death than in their own lifetime"[14]. It has been observed that Jeremiah's ministry was plagued by the fact that the failure of his prophecy of the enemy from the North to materialize seemed to prove at the very beginning that Jeremiah was a false prophet, so that the more he insisted on the imminence of the catastrophe, the more people jeered at him[15].

---

[11] See further C. C. Torrey, The Lives of the Prophets, 1946; and O. H. Steck, Israel und das gewaltsame Geschick der Propheten, 1967, who thinks of the tradition in Neh 9 26 as a theological rather than historical judgment.

[12] Israel, I—IV 1926 (1940). D. J. McCarthy, "Creation" Motifs in Ancient Hebrew Poetry, CBQ 29 (1967), 393—406, is sensitive to the difficulty of discerning at what point mythical elements lose their realism and come to be used as mere metaphors. For example, just how much of Isa 55 6-11 is metaphor is a difficult decision indeed.

[13] The Religion of Israel, 1960, 157f.

[14] Koheleth, the Man and His World, 1968, 23f., originally published in 1951.

[15] S. Frost, Patriarchs and Prophets, 1963, 170.

The relatively minor impact made by prophets upon their immediate hearers can be documented on page after page of the literature attributed to Amos, Hosea, Micah, Isaiah, Jeremiah, Ezekiel and Zechariah. A look at the first great classical prophet from this standpoint is instructive. Here it is said that the people made the Nazirites betray their vow not to drink wine and commanded the prophets to refrain from practicing their vocation (Am 2 12). Despite the message of judgment which Amos proclaimed to this people, they were persuaded that Yahweh was in their midst to deliver them from any harm (5 14 9 10), and eagerly anticipated the Day of the Lord (5 18-20, a day of battle or cultic festival)[16], for their religious zeal was beyond reproach.

Hosea's discovery that the prophet was a fool to the people came in spite of the religious interest of his contemporaries who showed their love by kissing the golden calves in the royal sanctuaries and offering lavish sacrifices (13 2 8 13), and who transgressed the law only to cry to Yahweh, "My God, we Israel know thee" (8 1 f.)[17]. His understanding of the judgmental role of prophecy implies, however, that its words have wreaked havoc (6 5). Hosea's younger contemporary Micah was confronted by a hostile audience who demanded that the prophet refrain from preaching judgment, for "disgrace will not overtake us" (2 6). He it is who informs us of a prophetic word that accorded with the reward offered (3 5), and who castigates priests and prophets for profiteering, and then in pious mood leaning upon the Lord and relying upon his presence and protection (3 9-11).

The prophet Isaiah understood his total ministry in terms of failure. Besides the important passage already mentioned (6 9-10), there are several in which the same point is made. The incident recorded in chapters 7—8 dealing with the so-called Syro-Ephraimitic war is typical; here the prophetic demand for faith is spurned and Isaiah's counsel ignored, leading some scholars to posit a long period of silence on Isaiah's part after this dismal failure. With biting sarcasm the mockery of the people is turned upon them in 28 7-13; here those who mock the prophet for childish talk will be forced to listen to the strange babble of a conquering army. Like soldiers facing their final

[16] G. von Rad, The Origin of the Concept of the Day of Jahweh, JSS 4 (1959), 97—108; F. C. Fensham, A Possible Origin of the Concept of the Day of the Lord, in: Biblical Essays, 1966, 90—97; and M. Weiss, The Origin of the "Day of the Lord" Reconsidered, HUCA 37 (1966), 29—60.

[17] H. W. Wolff, "Wissen um Gott" bei Hosea als Urform von Theologie, EvTh 12 (1952—53), 533—554 (reprinted in: Gesammelte Studien zum Alten Testament); J. L. McKenzie, Knowledge of God in Hosea, JBL 74 (1955), 22—27; and E. Baumann, "Wissen um Gott" bei Hosea als Urform der Theologie?, EvTh 15 (1955), 416—425.

battle with resignation (22 13), these people say in arrogance that their actions cannot be determined by Yahweh (5 15 f. 9 9 f.). Accordingly, they demand of seers and prophets their own illusions rather than the divine word (30 9-11). Small wonder the prophet Isaiah had no success with Hezekiah during the Philistine rebellion and the invasion of Sennacherib, prophetic legend to the contrary[18].

The vain effort on Jeremiah's part has been mentioned. In accord with his statement of wasted ministry the prophet refers to himself as a laughingstock (20 7 f.), the butt of every man's ridicule. Even during the reign of Zedekiah, who was less hostile than Jehoiakim and on occasion sought advice from Jeremiah, the situation is no different, for the king permits the pressure of officials around him to nullify the prophetic counsel (38 14 ff.). Likewise in the so-called idyllic period during the governorship of Gedaliah[19], there is little change, for the advice given those who slew the ruler is ignored (42 1 ff.). The situation is the same with Ezekiel, the prophet's failure being re-

[18] B. S. Childs, Isaiah and the Assyrian Crisis, 1967, has given a form-critical analysis of the prophetic oracles dealing with the vexing problem of Isaiah's role in the crisis brought about by Sennacherib's invasion of Judah, and has rejected both the extreme optimism of J. Bright, A History of Israel, 1959, 169—271. 282—287, and skepticism of S. H. Blank, Prophetic Faith in Isaiah, 1958. Bright's hypothesis regarding the actual historical events is well known, and demands little comment. He thinks there were two campaigns against Judah by Sennacherib, the first in 701, a major defeat for Judah, and the last in 688, the occasion of a disaster to the Assyrian army, and that both incidents have been telescoped into one by the prophetic account (cf. H. B. MacLean, Hezekiah, IDB II, 600, for a similar view). More probable, however, is M. Noth's position of only *one* campaign, and that in 701 (The History of Israel, 1958, 267—269; cf. A. L. Oppenheim, Sennacherib, IDB IV, 270—272, who points out that a general rebellion would have accompanied any such epidemic, and there was none). The question of Isaiah's message during this crisis is difficult, but has been discussed most helpfully by von Rad (Old Testament Theology II 155—169). The prominence of the Zion tradition of threat and eleventh-hour divine deliverance in the message of Isaiah, together with the narrative in II Sam 24, provide an adequate explanation for the tradition of Zion's inviolability, and the place of "faith" in genuine oracles of Isaiah distinguishes them from the legendary material in chapters 36—39. Von Rad's observation that not one of Isaiah's great Zion sayings came true, and his attempt to understand Isa 22 4 in terms of the prophet's bitter disappointment with the people (not Yahweh, despite the hardening of their hearts!) for not having faith in the moment to which Isaiah had looked forward all his life are particularly poignant (166 f.). The significance of faith to Isaiah has been recognized most clearly by G. Fohrer, Introduction to the Old Testament, 373 note 35, who writes: "No unconditional promise of salvation can be found in Isaiah (Blank, Vriezen, Whitley), such a promise can only be put together out of the optimistic utterances inserted later into the book." This provides a necessary corrective to von Rad's emphasis on Isaiah's positive word for Zion regardless of the human response.

[19] J. Skinner, Prophecy and Religion, 1922, 272—284.

flected in the refrain "When this comes — and come it will! — then they will know that a prophet has been among them" (33 33), reminiscent of Isaiah's "Behold, I and the children whom the Lord has given me are signs and portents in Israel from the Lord of Hosts, who dwells in Zion" (8 18).

The prophet Zechariah underscores the failure of the "former prophets" who urged Israel to return from her evil deeds, only to be met with negative response, and asks if the prophets live forever (1 4 f.). In another place he refers to the earlier period of prosperity when the message of the former prophets questioned the necessity of the cult and urged morality instead; on this occasion, however, the people "refused to hearken, and turned a stubborn shoulder, and stopped their ears that they might not hear. They made their hearts like adamant lest they should hear the law and the words which the Lord of hosts had sent by his Spirit through the former prophets" (7 7-12).

### *The Chronicler's Ideal View*

The situation is strikingly different in Chronicles, where prophets are often said to have been successful in their dealings with royalty. The motto of the Chronicler in this regard may be found in II Chr 20 20, where it is written that the highly revered Levites departed into the wilderness of Tekoa, and Jehoshaphat stood and said, "Hear me, Judah and inhabitants of Jerusalem! Believe in the Lord your God, and you will be established; believe his prophets, and you will succeed". Three examples illustrate this conviction of the author. In II Chr 12 5-8 the prophet Shemaiah pronounces a word of destruction for Rehoboam, but reverses it when the princes and king humble themselves and proclaim a brief doxology of judgment[20]. Nonetheless, the

---

[20] The term was shown to be useful in understanding the doxologies of Amos by F. Horst, Die Doxologien im Amosbuch, ZAW 48 (1929), 45—54 (reprinted in: Gottes Recht 1961), Horst viewed the doxologies as a hymn of two strophies, each with identical concluding refrain ("Yahweh is his name" and "Who calls for the waters of the sea, and pours them upon the surface of the earth"), and argued for a *Sitz im Leben* in sacral law, the accused confessing his guilt and praising the punishing Judge. Besides parallels from the history of religions, Horst called attention to Josh 7 19 (where Achan is admonished to confess his guilt and praise Yahweh) Job 4—5 (5 8 refers to a trial, while 5 9-16 constitutes a hymnic doxology) Jer 13 15f. I Sam 6 5 Ps 118 17-21 and I Chr 30 8 (LXX). The confession of sins in connection with the doxologies of Amos is said to be 4 6-11 and 9 1-4, the latter more in the nature of a description of the chastisement. Both von Rad (Old Testament Theology I 357 ff.) and R. Knierim (The Vocation of Isaiah, VT 18, 1968, 56) accept the concept, and add other passages to be viewed from this perspective (I Kings 8 33 Ezr 10 7ff. Dan 3 31-34 Neh 9 Ezr 6 Dan 9 Isa 12 1f., so von Rad; and Ps 16 56-60 29 1-9 89 7-15

author feels it necessary to point out that repentance did not remove the threat of invasion entirely, for Shishak ravages the land. His remark that repentance made the devastation less than complete, and "moreover, conditions were good in Judah" (12 12) shows how forced his interpretation of the incident really was. Similarly, II Chr 15 1-19 tells of a successful appeal by a prophet named Azariah the son of Oded, and of Asa's subsequent removal of all abominable idols from the land of Judah and Benjamin, the restoration of the altar of the Lord in front of the Temple, and the covenant entered into by the people to put to death anyone who refused to seek the God of Israel. But the sequel to this story admits that things were not always so good for prophets, Asa becoming angry with Hanani the seer and putting him in the stocks, in prison (II Chr 16 7-10). In II Chr 28 8-15 a prophet named Oded confronts the army of Israel that had taken captive and brought to Samaria a sizable group of kinsfolk; Oded warns the captors that they have sins enough without adding to them the subjugation of people of Jerusalem and Judah as slaves. In this instance the prophet is backed by a number of chiefs, and the captives clothed, fed, anointed, and taken to Jericho. The Chronicler was aware, however, that the prophetic witness was often frustrated, and illustrates this with a provocative story about an unknown prophet who denounced Amaziah for worshipping the god of the Edomites. The king refuses to listen, advising the prophet that silence will save his life: "Have we made you a royal counselor?[21] Stop! Why should you be put to death?" (II Chr 25 14-46).

### *Cultic Prayers*

This study of the prophetic impact upon Israelite society would not be complete without a glance at the role of prophecy as seen in

---

118 17-21 I Sam 6 5 Jer 13 15f. Mic 1 1 Isa 6 3, so Knierim). The writer has sought to show that the doxology of judgment and prophetic recitation of disciplinary punishment characteristic of ancient days of penitence gave way in the exilic and post-exilic community to hymnic confessions concluded by the refrain "Yahweh of hosts is his name" (Jer 10 12-16 31 35 51 15-19 Isa 51 15), and finally to cultic confessional prayers (Dan 9 Neh 9 Ezr 9 Jer 32). See *YHWH Ṣebaʾôt Šemô*: A Form-Critical Analysis, ZAW 81 (1969), 156—175. In this context the striking emphasis upon a theophany of judgment may be mentioned, along with the frequent presence of *baraʾ* (see the long footnote 66 of the article cited in the previous sentence). Finally, II Chr 12 6 should be added to the passages belonging to this discussion of the doxology of judgment.

[21] P. A. H. de Boer, The Counsellor, in: Wisdom in Israel and in the Ancient Near East, 1960, 42—71; and W. McKane, Prophets and Wise Men, 1965. The suicide of Ahithophel (II Sam 17 23) indicates how serious the business of advising a king was.

late cultic prayers, specifically Dan 9 Ezr 9 and Neh 9. These prayers contain a striking similarity of language and content, and view prophecy from the same standpoint. In every instance the concern is to exalt Yahweh as just and merciful, and to confess the sin of disobedience and failure to heed the commandments spoken by the prophets.

The prayer in Dan 9 confesses that Israel has not "listened to thy servants the prophets, who spoke in thy name to our kings, our princes, and our fathers, and to all the people of the land" (9 6), and admits to not having followed God's laws "which he set before his servants the prophets" (9 10). Consequently, it is recognized that while to the Lord belong mercy and forgiveness, to sinful Israelites belongs confusion of face in terms of the curse and oath written in the Mosaic legislation, which Yahweh has confirmed by bringing a great calamity (cf. Jer 32 24).

Ezr 9 also confesses that Israel has rebelled against God's servants the prophets, even if identifying the content of the divine statutes transmitted by them as restrictions against intermarriage with foreigners, an offense being repeated in Ezra's day. Prophetic theology is also echoed in this prayer, particularly the idea of a remnant that has been spared by the God before whom none can stand because of guilt.

Most significant, however, is Neh 9, where the treatment given the prophets is mentioned in striking fashion. Here one finds a lengthy account of *Heilsgeschichte*, together with the recognition that the people of God rebelled against his goodness and killed the prophets who warned them to return to Yahweh, for which sin Israel had been given into the hands of her enemies, but had been delivered after crying to Yahweh for assistance. It is said that for many years God bore with the rebellious people, warning them by his Spirit through the prophets, "yet they would not give ear" (9 30). The exile, then, was to be expected, but still God spared a remnant. Hardship is said to have fallen upon kings, princes, priests, *prophets*, fathers and all the people, whereas guilt lay on kings, princes, priests and fathers! The absence of prophets in this list of offenders is particularly striking (contrast Lam 4 13), especially in view of the numerous attacks on prophets in Jeremiah and Ezekiel. The prayer concludes with the observation that Yahweh has punished the sinners with bondage, a kind of hidden appeal for deliverance.

In brief, the cultic prayers, permeated as they are by the Deuteronomic style and theology, look back upon the prophets as transmitters and proclaimers of the laws of God, and interpret Israel's response as constant rebellion and even murder. Here again the failure of prophecy confronts the reader, and confirms the basic argument above.

Von Rad has called attention to a factor that forces one to recognize, however, that prophetic words did on occasion take root. This is the presence in Chronicles of levitical sermons in which the prophetic word of an earlier day is quoted and given new application (cf. II Chr 20 20 and Isa 7 9)[22]. Nevertheless, O. Plöger has correctly perceived the guardian role of prophecy according to the Chronicler, one in which the community based on Mosaic law was the goal, and once achieved, left no place for prophecy[23]. Indeed, Chronicles is opposed to prophetic theology which looks forward to the promises of Yahweh, for to this author the ideal theocracy is present reality[24]. Two other factors indicate, however, that the prophetic witness was not entirely fruitless, the presence of a canon of prophetic literature and the existence of prophetic traditionists, whether disciples, sons or what. Both the presence of those who kept traditions of prophetic words until their fulfillment or new relevance because of the course of history, and the eventual veneration of select tradition-complexes can only mean that the prophetic witness found fertile soil, even if only in a remnant of faithful Israelites who perceived the hand of God in the Babylonian captivity, and who understood the earlier fall of Israel and that of Judah as confirmation of the message of certain prophets, namely those who proclaimed a word of judgment.

The presence of Deuteronomic language in prophetic books, particularly Amos and Jeremiah[25], raises the possibility of prophetic influence upon Deuteronomy and those responsible for its promulgation. Although it has been generally assumed that the social ethics permeating the book owes its origin to prophetic circles[26], this view has recently been challenged in favor of a wisdom background for the humanitarian interests[27]. Given the prominent place of concern for the poor, widows and orphans in wisdom literature of Egypt and Mesopotamia, it is impossible to accept Hammershaimb's argument that Israelite prophecy has Canaanite origins since it shares with Ugaritic literature an interest in the welfare of widows, orphans and the poor[28]. In a word, such concern was felt by sages as well as prophets.

[22] The Levitical Sermon in I and II Chronicles, in: The Problem of the Hexateuch and other Essays 274, originally in: Festschrift für O. Procksch, 1934.

[23] Theocracy and Eschatology, 1968, 42.

[24] W. Rudolph, Chronikbücher, 1955, XXIII.

[25] W. H. Schmidt, Die deuteronomistische Redaktion des Amosbuches, ZAW 77 (1965), 168—192; and J. P. Hyatt, The Deuteronomic Edition of Jeremiah, Vanderbilt Studies in the Humanities 1 (1951), 71—95, as well as most treatments of Jeremiah (Rudolph, Weiser — somewhat differently).

[26] Fohrer, Introduction to the Old Testament, 174.

[27] M. Weinfeld, The Origin of Humanism in Deuteronomy, and Deuteronomy — The Present State of Inquiry, JBL 80 (1961), 241—247, and 86 (1967), 249—262.

[28] Some Aspects of Old Testament Prophecy from Isaiah to Malachi 71—75. See rather F. C. Fensham, Widow, Orphan, and the Poor in Ancient Near Eastern Legal and Wisdom Literature, JNES 21 (1962), 129—139.

The prophetic influence upon Deuteronomy may be described as an unusual one, as von Rad has recognized. If one refuses to follow him in the thesis that Deuteronomy is the product of so-called false prophets, one must at least admit that the attitude to prophetic conduct in Deuteronomy is rather strange. This is evident in the fact that the book insists on the criterion of fulfillment for the oracle of woe, whereas Jeremiah applies it to a message of weal, as well as in the harsh treatment to be meted out to the erring or apostasizing prophet (13 1ff. 18 19-22). Moreover, the well-known passage in Dtn 18 15 f. implies that there has been no true prophet like Moses to the time of the composition of Deuteronomy, unless the Hebrew is understood to mean that from time to time the Lord will raise up prophets like Moses[29]. Finally, it may be asked whether the legalistic tone, centralization of worship, and trend toward a "religion of the Book" do not render any hypothesis of prophetic influence questionable.

In a word, the impact of prophecy upon Israelite society was negligible, especially when compared with the later veneration of the prophet and expectation of an eschatological era when "the prophet" would herald the coming of the Lord. This thesis of a failure of prophecy is little affected by the presence of small conventicles who preserved prophetic words and applied them to new situations, nor is it obviated by the elevation of prophecy to the "unattainable and always future", a trend characteristic of post-exilic Judaism. An explanation for this failure of prophecy must be sought, and the responsibility placed at the feet of prophet or hearer.

### *Reasons for the Failure*

It has been observed above that the essential weakness of prophecy was its lack of any means of validating a message claimed to be of divine origin. The prophets themselves were cognizant of their vulnerability at this point and devised means of safe-guarding themselves from the charge of misrepresentation. The mere claim to be a spokesman of God contained within the messenger formula, *kō 'amăr 'ᵃdonay*, or the oracular formula, *nᵉ'um 'ᵃdonay*, was early recognized to be insufficient substantiation to a doubting populace. Consequently, additional means of convincing the people were utilized, namely call auditions and visions, appeal to the fulfillment or the character of the message, as well as to the behavior of the bearer of that word in adversity, the argument from tradition, and external signs. Furthermore, argumentation comes to occupy a major place in the prophetic mes-

[29] Muilenburg, The "Office" of the Prophet in Ancient Israel, 88, prefers this interpretation.

sage, particularly in Jeremiah and Ezekiel, and is taken up into pedagogy in the book of Malachi. It must be admitted that the tone of much of this self-vindication militated against the communication of a word; here the difference between prophetic disputations and contest literature in wisdom texts is maximal, the latter functioning well as an instructive device[30]. From the oracles of Ezekiel one gets the impression that he thought God was also aware of the absence of any validation for his word, so that we hear the refrain *ad nauseum*, "Then you shall know that I am the Lord". The contexts of these refrains indicate that such knowledge will be the result of some *spectacular act* on God's part, thus high-lighting the difficulty facing a prophet who could not depend on a "shattering" experience to persuade his hearers.

Nowhere is this lack of validation more noticeable than at the point of the prophetic interpretation of history. Indeed, Frost's contention that the burden which prophetic religion placed upon history was greater than it could bear provides a plausible explanation for the apocalyptist's return to mythology[31]. His delineation of the basic problems raised by the prophetic interpretation of history in terms of disagreement between prophets who saw the historical situation differently, prolonged oppression of the people of God, and an excessively long "frame of history" can hardly be off target[32]. Furthermore, the liturgical pieces of "negative historical retrospect" interspersed within

[30] This contest literature usually has a mythological introduction, followed by a debate between two contestants, the resolution of which is determined by divine judgment. The prophetic disputation has little in common with these literary works, for nowhere is there a mythological setting, personification of nature or animals, or a divine judgment scene. On the contrary, prophetic disputes are between real persons and reflect a situation of actual conflict. Furthermore, the wisdom disputation has as its purpose the discussion of the relative value of things, animals or professions, whereas the prophetic concern is theological, indeed a matter of life and death. Hence the mood of the wisdom dispute is playful, while a sombre note hangs over the prophetic disputation. Again the wisdom genre is employed by students or scribes among whom there is basic agreement, but the opponents in the prophetic dispute are at polar extremes, so that a degree of heat is generated in the discussion that militates against the success of the prophet — unless perhaps his sole purpose in using the device is to vindicate his ministry rather than to persuade his opponents. See especially Lambert, Babylonian Wisdom Literature, 151—211; and E. I. Gordon, A New Look at the Wisdom of Sumer and Akkad, BiOr 17 (1960), 144—147.

[31] S. B. Frost, Apocalyptic and History, in: The Bible in Modern Scholarship 98—113.

[32] Ibid. 112 ("We may conclude, then, that so far from being the first philosophers of history, the apocalyptists are in fact a school of biblical writers who recognized that the burden which Hebrew religion had laid upon history was greater than it could bear"). Later we shall call attention to a similar situation in current biblical theology where the burden placed on history has once again been too heavy.

prophetic oracles[33] and in Psalms indicate that the recitation of saving history had its counterpart in retributive history, even if something of the odium of the passages is removed by viewing the punishment as disciplinary.

Frost's second point, prolonged oppression of the covenanted people, is another way of putting the problem of the justice of God, a subject that is central to our discussion above. Confronted with the apparent injustice of God, Israel responded in four ways: (1) she confessed God's healing presence in the face of everything; (2) she found comfort in the prophetic promise that God would soon act decisively; (3) she gloried in the grandeur of creation, confessing that creaturely silence is mandatory[34]; or (4) she uttered a sceptical cry of despair (Qoheleth). It is noteworthy that these answers are taken from apocalyptic and wisdom [and psalmnic] literature, a point to which we shall return shortly.

Still another explanation for the failure of prophecy may be seen in the nature of the religious community after the return from Babylonian exile. In a theocratic society there is neither necessity nor place for a prophetic office, for it is assumed that the will of God is already operative. This understanding of the guardian role of prophecy goes a long way in explaining the prophetic narratives in Chronicles (and, incidentally, the dearth of prophecy in the Solomonic era), and provides something of the rationale behind the veneration of *past* prophets.

Just as the changed religious situation affected the course of prophecy negatively, so also did the sociological transition during the exilic and post-exilic period. The adverse influence of emerging individualism has already been discussed, and here it need only be said that the result was an identification between the prophet and his office so that an attack upon the one was an affront to the other. Again, mention should be made of the pervasive nationalistic spirit characteristic of post-exilic Judaism which left its stamp upon prophecy, as shown in ironic fashion by the Jonah legend[35]. Finally, lest it be overlooked, the fact that prophecy and monarchy were almost co-terminus, a factor far too infrequently noted, indicates that sociological factors must not be ignored in assessing the demise of classical prophecy.

To sum up, various reasons led to the failure of prophecy, graphically illustrated by Zech 13 2-6. The irony of this passage is that appeal

---

[33] The author has examined two of these liturgical passages in A Liturgy of Wasted Opportunity (Am 4 6-12 Isa 9 7—10 4 5 25-29), Sem 1 (1970), 27—37.

[34] W. Eichrodt, Vorsehungsglaube und Theodizee im Alten Testament, in: Festschrift O. Procksch, 1934, 64—70.

[35] M. Burrows, The Literary Category of the Book of Jonah, in: Translating and Understanding the Old Testament (H. G. May Festschrift), 1970, 80—107, prefers to view the book as a satire.

for the eradication of the prophetic voice echoes Amos' well-known response to Amaziah (*lo' nabî' 'anokî*), and in the very process of ruling out prophecy as a present valid means of religious expression the author invariably shows his indebtedness to prophecy. Thus the curious fact that prophets are both silenced and venerated stares us in the face, both here and in other late literature (cultic prayers, Chronicles).

## B. WISDOM AND APOCALYPTIC FILL THE VOID

It was observed above that the answers given to the problem of divine injustice come from apocalyptic and wisdom literature. Once prophecy was shown to be incapable of bearing the burden of history, unable to validate itself in the present, and unwilling to deal with the problem of evil save in apodictic fashion, a void appeared in Israel's soul. Neither apocalyptic nor wisdom suffered from the above weaknesses, and both rushed in to fill the vacancy.

The burden of history is overcome by apocalyptic's return to mythology and stance of expectancy. The emphasis upon the transcendental world, with its accompanying angelic intermediaries, shifted the focus from the kingdoms of this world, all of which were beastly save one (the Hasmonean). At the same time, the eschatological tenor of the message was such as to avoid the embarrassment of history *for a season, at least*[36]. Regardless of the external circumstances it could be argued that God was *preparing to act*, a claim beyond question, and one that was far more realistic than prophecy's dogma about God's control of history for the accomplishing of His ends. The progressive deterioration of society, as evidenced by the prosperity of the wicked and poverty of the righteous, only confirmed apocalyptic's thesis of God's withdrawal from the arena of history, a theme that was not entirely foreign to prophecy[37].

---

[36] There is a sense, however, in which apocalyptic fell victim to its claims about the in-breaking of divine activity, for despite valiant efforts on the part of the faithful to defeat God's enemies, the expected assistance from above failed to materialize. This fact eventually leads to the demise of apocalyptic, despite occasional resurgences when the course of history becomes particularly oppressive.

[37] Cf. Am 8 11-14 7 8 8 1 f. Hos 5 6 9 12 Mic 3 7 Isa 45 15 ("Truly, thou art a God who hidest thyself, O God of Israel, the Savior"). A. Heschel, Man Is Not Alone, 1951, 153, emphasizes the fact that in the prophetic view God is not hidden but *hiding*. K. Miskotte, When the Gods are Silent, 1967, recognizes the power of this concept both for biblical and contemporary theology, even if focusing upon the silence of *pagan* gods permitting the *Name* to rise above us as it did over Abraham, Moses, David and countless persons unnamed (115).

The issue of authority was addressed by apocalyptic in a rather surprising way, namely the artifice of pseudonymity. By means of this literary device apocalyptic was able to put forth new religious views clothed in the authority of ancient worthies (Enoch, Adam, Elijah, Moses, Daniel, etc.) against whom none would cavil. Even the transcendence of God contributed to the authority of apocalyptic, since angelic mediation assumed a place of primary significance. Accordingly the dream, so debatable in prophetic circles during the sixth century, becomes the chief revelatory vehicle of apocalyptic.

The problem of evil was not shunned by apocalyptic, for the belief in demonic powers operative in the present and in an innate tendency to sinfulness provided an adequate explanation for human suffering, particularly when coupled with the conviction that adversity was disciplinary, that hardship was a purging of dross from the pure metal of one's character. Particularly fortunate was the apocalyptist's ability to shift the scene of reward to the next world, for this meant that innocent suffering is no decisive argument against the justice of God inasmuch as death is not the final word. Here we find the preservation of the message of the so-called false prophets, namely *šalôm*, even if the time-table has been lengthened drastically. By means of this promise that, despite every experience that would seem to deny God's goodness, God's plans for his people are going to be brought to fruition, the apocalyptist continued one line of prophecy. Indeed, even the prophet of doom may have envisioned salvation beyond judgment, so that between apocalyptic and prophecy there is not an unsurpassable gulf[38].

The wisdom movement was also flexible enough to deal with the unsolved problems of prophecy. History poses no real threat because her own interest and claims, while historical[39], do not presuppose something about history that cannot be substantiated. Indeed, the incorporation of sacred history (and legal traditions) does not occur until the second century with Sirach and Wisdom of Solomon[40], wisdom's domain being rather the universal phenomena, yea creation itself[41]. And even sacred history in these late works is of past occurrences, so that history never becomes a source of embarrassment to the sage.

---

[38] P. von der Osten-Sacken, Die Apokalyptik in ihrem Verhältnis zu Prophetie und Weisheit, 1969.

[39] H. H. Schmid, Wesen und Geschichte der Weisheit, 1966, 4ff. and passim.

[40] J. Fichtner, Zum Problem Glaube und Geschichte in der israelitisch-jüdischen Weisheitsliteratur, ThLZ 76 (1951), 145—150 (Gottes Weisheit, 1965, 9—17).

[41] W. Zimmerli, Ort und Grenze der Weisheit im Rahmen alttestamentlicher Theologie, in: Les Sagesses du Proche-Orient ancien 121—137, translated into English in SJTh 58 (1964), 146—158.

Again, the problem of authority does not seem to have arisen in wisdom circles, despite the fact that the sage spoke with the authority of the past testimony to human and divine nature. The authority of the sage was that of the Creator himself, hence the prominence of the twin concepts of the *fear of* and *will of* God. Indeed, only Wisdom can invite people to come to her, can speak a message of selfhood; both prophet and priest can only point man beyond themselves. Even the motivation clauses within wisdom literature call attention to the authoritative character of the sage, whose function is to instruct king and subject. Finally, the formula "Listen, my son, to your father's advice" carries with it the authority of a father who has control over life and limb. This authority, however, is not manifested with a heavy hand, for wisdom has place for contradictory statements side by side[42].

Wisdom can never be accused of side-stepping the problem of evil, for her own dogma of individual retribution intensified the problem of innocent suffering. Hence we are not surprised to discover within her ranks those who continue the sceptical mood of the populace, profound thinkers who probe the depths of reality itself (Job and Qoheleth). The marvel is the co-existence of such contrasting approaches to the solution of the problem of evil, the "mystical" escape to God's presence in Job and the mildly eudaemonistic scepticism of Qoheleth. It should be noted that Job is not free of prophetic influence[43], both stylistically and theologically, so that the continuity between Job and prophecy cannot be denied, at least in the resolution of the problem of human suffering. Furthermore, wisdom's experiential rather than apodictic stance provided a point of contact with the people, a linkage rarely found in prophecy.

To conclude, the conflict between prophets so degraded the prophetic movement that its witness was weakened, and prophetic theology was too burdensome to overcome such a weakness. Small wonder the prophets are honored and silenced. But the voice of prophecy was not completely silent, its emphases being taken up into apocalyptic and wisdom, in both of which there is willingness to wrestle with the problem of divine injustice, and in neither of which there is a claim about

---

[42] Zimmerli's position that wisdom's council was devoid of authority (Zur Struktur der alttestamentlichen Weisheit, especially 181—189. 194—203) has been challenged from a number of quarters recently. See B. Gemser, The Spiritual Structure of Biblical Aphoristic Wisdom, Homiletica en Biblica 21 (1962), 3—10 (Adhuc Loquitur, 1968, 138—149); P. A. H. de Boer, The Counsellor, 56. 65. 71; U. Skladny, Die ältesten Spruchsammlungen in Israel, 1962, 89ff.; W. McKane, Prophets and Wise Men, 48 and passim; Proverbs, 1970, 59. 75—78. 119—121. 155; K. Bauer-Kayatz, Einführung in die alttestamentliche Weisheit, 1969, 33f. 40f. 58ff., especially 95.

[43] N. H. Snaith, The Book of Job, 1968, 33.

history that experience soon proved untrue. The fact that wisdom and apocalyptic address themselves to the major problems facing prophecy, and that they continue many prophetic themes, further confirms our suspicion that we have compartmentalized Israelite society far too often. Such separating of prophet, priest and sage into neat categories so that influence of the one upon the other is proof of official "membership or schooling" rather than common participation in the ills of a society cannot longer be maintained.

# Conclusion

Our discussion of prophetic conflict and its effect upon Israelite religion has arrived at the conclusion that tension within prophetic circles derives from the nature of prophecy itself, that is, from the two-fold task of the reception of the word of God in the experience of divine mystery, and the articulation of that word to man in all its nuances and with persuasive cogency. G. Fohrer has perceived this fact clearly; he writes: "Schließlich erkennen wir nun, wie falsche Prophetie entsteht. Entweder liegt überhaupt keine geheime Erfahrung zugrunde, so daß alles Gesagte völlig in der Luft hängt, oder die geheime Erfahrung ist vom Propheten in falscher Weise gedeutet, ausgelegt oder verstandesmäßig bearbeitet worden"[1].

But we were also forced to conclude that prophetic tension cannot be explained solely in anthropological categories, for the likelihood of conflict within biblical prophecy was enhanced by the belief that Yahweh made use of men against their will or knowledge to accomplish his intentions, indeed on occasion sent deceptive visions to further the divine purpose for Israel. In essence, then, human limitation and divine sovereignty combined to create prophetic conflict.

Since these factors compelled the prophets to engage in a life-and-death struggle, it was imperative that they equip themselves for the battle. The tragedy of their existence was a failure to come up with an adequate means of self-validation that would lend weight to their authoritative word devoid of any means of authentication. Not a single one of the numerous criteria proposed for this purpose functioned in the present moment (cf. I Kings 13) either for the prophet or for his hearers, both of whom needed to know whether a spoken word carried any more weight than the authority of its bearer. The result was increased polarization of prophet against prophet, and people against prophet, followed by claim and counter-claim, self-assertion and inner turmoil.

Such internal debate was heightened by the nature of the prophetic message, which contributed to the tension because of its diversity and its claim about history that was not borne out in daily experience.

---

[1] Die Propheten des Alten Testaments im Blickfeld neuer Forschung, in: Studien zur alttestamentlichen Prophetie (1949—1965), 1967, 9f. (originally in: Das Wort im evangelischen Religionsunterricht, 1954—55, 15—24).

Unfortunately for the movement itself, prophecy did not possess the flexibility to face its own contradictions, the disparity between theology and experience. Consequently the public itself found prophecy lacking and turned elsewhere for spiritual direction, namely to apocalyptic and wisdom, both of which wrestle with the problem of evil and are somewhat less of a slave to crippling presuppositions. But this was not a total rejection of prophecy, for an impact had been made upon a small group of followers responsible for the preservation of the prophetic literature and among whom there was the anticipation of the return of prophecy at a later time, and within wisdom and apocalyptic many emphases of prophetic theology found expression.

It is somewhat ironical that current biblical theology finds itself in a comparable situation with ancient prophecy, having laid upon history a burden too great for it to bear. The modern trend to seek a solution to the excessive emphasis upon "the mighty acts of God in history"[2] in a theology of hope or in wisdom literature, which is thought to be more compatible with a humanistic society[3], indicates that human nature changes little over the millennia[4], for this is precisely the approach followed by ancient Israel when the claims about God's control of history were called into question by the process of history itself.

---

[2] Discussed recently by B. Childs, Biblical Theology in Crisis, 1970.

[3] It is doubly ironical that the latest studies in wisdom literature challenge the traditional view that wisdom is non-authoritarian. See Excursus B for an analysis of the recent trend.

[4] Perhaps this fact is also a positive good. Our analysis of "false prophecy" demands that each of us look within his own life for the lie, since "even the wisest and most profound of us holds but a glimpse of truth, treasured alongside many a false notion, many a prejudice, many a downright lie" (S. Frost, Patriarchs and Prophets, 211), and once he finds cosmos and chaos in himself, he is "faced with a permanent threat of chaos, but equally permanent is the possibility of encounter with the creative God, who overcomes chaos, and hence the possibility of defeating the dragon and inaugurating peace" (V. Maag, The Antichrist as a Symbol of Evil, in: Evil, ed. Jung Institute Curatorium, 1967, 80).

# Excursus A: False Prophecy in the New Testament Period

K. Harms has discerned a kind of unity of the Bible in the phenomenon of false prophecy[1], for this problem is common to both Testaments. Such was to be expected, for the Christian literature is also the product of human beings limited by their *Weltanschauung*, ethical commitment, geographical setting, and mental ability, is indeed broken testimony.

In some quarters it was believed that the Holy Spirit ceased to inspire men after the time of Ezra, which amounts to a cessation of prophecy. B. Sotah 48b states that after Haggai, Zechariah and Malachi the Holy Spirit ceased to be active in Israel, while B. Ber. 34b reports that "after the destruction of the temple prophecy was taken from the prophets and given to the wise." The latter point is also made in B. Bath. 12a and J. Ber. 3b, 26, in both of which the prophetic spirit is said to have passed to the scribes. In a slightly different vein Josephus writes that the three charismata of ancient Israel (prophecy, kingship, and priesthood) now rest upon the Hasmonaeans under John Hyrcanus.[2] The polemical aspect of this hypothesis about the withdrawal of the Holy Spirit has long been noted, for it is a means of refuting Christian claims about the inspiration of Jesus and his followers.

The disappearance of prophecy, understandable in terms of Zech 13 2-6, is thought by many modern critics to lie behind I Macc 4 45f. 9 27 and 14 41. The first passage tells of the restoration of the defiled sanctuary under Judas, and of the decision to tear down the altar of burnt offering and to store the stones in a convenient place "until there should come a prophet to tell what to do with them." The second, 9 27, refers to a time of great distress "such as had not been since the time that prophets ceased to appear among them." I Macc 14 41 states that the people decided upon Simon as "their leader and high priest forever, until a trustworthy prophet should arise . . ." (cf. Ps 74 9 and Prayer of Azariah 15).

It is generally concluded on the basis of these passages that prophecy had died out, but such a view is difficult to maintain. More correct is the thesis that in some circles prophecy was relegated to the past, but in others the prophetic witness was still very much alive (for example, at Qumran,[3] and in the person of John the Baptist, Jesus

[1] Die falschen Propheten: Eine biblische Untersuchung 56.

[2] Jewish Antiquities, xiii, 10, 7. For discussion of the issue in question, see Plöger, Theocracy and Eschatology, 23f. and 42; Foerster, From the Exile to Christ, 4—5, and Der heilige Geist im sog. Spätjudentum, in: De Spiritu Sancto, 1964, 40ff.; E. Fascher, Prophétes, 1927, 161—164; and O. Cullmann, The Christology of the New Testament, 1959, 13—50, especially 14—23.

[3] Where the conflict between the "Teacher of Righteousness" and the "Prophet of Falsehood" brings into sharp focus the question of false prophecy. It may be noted that the Hodayot give evidence of the conviction that prophetic inspiration is a living reality to the author(s). The Manual of Discipline views the community as prophetic in principle and looks for an eschatological prophet (8 1ff. 9 10f.), while false prophets

of Nazareth, numerous messianic claimants, and in the Christian movement). It may be observed that the prophetic quality of the ministries of John and Jesus was clear to all, and that early Christian literature assumes the existence of prophecy both in Judaism and in its offshoot, Christianity (Acts 13 4-12 11 28 21 10-14 I Cor 12 10 13 2. 9-10 etc.). It is to be noted, however, that a Christian prophet was more of a teacher or preacher whose task was to edify the congregation.[4]

There is a sense, however, in which the anticipation of the coming of one final prophet at the *éschaton* rendered any prophetic voice of the present moment somewhat ineffective. This expectation of an eschatological prophet, already present in Mal 4 5f., assumed many forms, or rather, was connected with various prophetic personalities. Accordingly, the final prophet was thought to be Moses, Elijah, Enoch, Jeremiah, or an angel.[5]

Prophecy in the New Testament was also made ineffective by the presence of false prophets, and the concomitant inability of the populace to discern the true from the false. There is evidence of increasing concern over the phenomenon of false prophecy, and the polemic is exceptionally caustic, perhaps because of the high veneration of genuine prophecy, and certainly because of a trend toward an intellectualistic understanding of the faith. The extent to which prophecy was held in esteem stands out rather visibly in Matthew, not only in the well-known formula of the fulfillment of prophecy (1 22 2 5. 15. 17. 23 3 3 4 14 8 17 12 17 13 35 21 4 24 15 26 59 27 9. 35), but also in incidental remarks (23 29f. 34. 36 22 40 21 26 16 14 13 17 11 9. 13 5 12. 17 7 12). This veneration of prophecy is almost equalled by Luke, and extends to Revelation, where the prophets are especially honored as martyrs for Christ (16 6 11 3-13). Moreover, the "gnostic heresy" within the early church, specifically the emphasis upon right belief rather than conduct, resulted in bitter attacks upon any who would pervert the belief of Christians, and introduced an element of hostility not present even in Jeremiah.

False prophecy is an issue in several passages in the New Testament, as well as in extra-canonical literature. In Mt 7 15f. the followers of Jesus are warned against false prophets who come in sheep's clothing but inwardly are ravenous wolves, while 24 24 predicts the rise of false prophets and false Christs who will lead astray the elect. Similarly, II Pet 2 1 speaks of false prophets among the people, just as false teachers walk among them, denying the Master. An echo of Old Testament indictments is heard

---

are recognized as a special problem to Qumran (The Damascus Code 8 1f.; Hodayot 4 9f. 2 31 4 16. 20). It has even been suggested that the so-called Dead Sea Scrolls were gathered as writings of false prophets and hidden by authority of Rabbi Simeon ben Gamaliel I (so M. Burrows, The Dead Sea Scrolls, 1955, 75).

[4] See R. Bowlin, The Christian Prophets in the New Testament, unpublished Ph. D. Dissertation, Vanderbilt University, 1958; H. A. Guy, New Testament Prophecy, 1947; and the literature cited in J. Mánek, Propheten, Biblisch-Historisches Handwörterbuch, 1512.

[5] See the helpful discussions of P. Volz, Die Eschatologie der jüdischen Gemeinde im neutestamentlichen Zeitalter, 1966 (originally 1934), 193—203; Cullmann, The Christology of the New Testament, 14—23; and J. Giblet, Prophétisme et attente d'un Messie prophète dans l'ancien Judaïsme, in: L'Attente du Messie (Coppens Festschrift, 1954) 85—130. It should be added that the Samaritans expected an eschatological figure, *Ta'eb*, clearly a Moses redivivus.

in I Thess 5 3, which warns against those who preach security (cf. *šalôm*) when sudden destruction will befall them. I Jn 4 1 warns that many false prophets have gone out, and urges Christians to test the spirits, while Rev 16 13 reports that demons issued forth from the mouth of the false prophet, and 19 20 describes the capture of this enemy who had worked signs to deceive those who received the mark of the beast. But perhaps most interesting is the legend in Acts 13 4-12, where Saul, Barnabas and John Mark encounter a Jewish false prophet at Paphos. This man, Bar-Jesus, a companion of the proconsul, Sergius Paulus, seeks to dissuade the Roman official from the faith and incurs the hostility of *Paul*, who calls *Elymas* the "son of the devil", an "enemy of all righteousness, full of all deceit and villainy" and strikes him with temporary blindness.

The Didache contains a fascinating passage dealing with false prophets (11 3-12). E. J. Goodspeed translates it as follows:[6] About apostles and prophets, follow the rule of the Gospel, which is this: Let every apostle who comes to you be welcomed as the Lord. But he shall not stay more than one day, and if it is necessary, the next day also. But if he stays three days, he is a false prophet. And when an apostle leaves, let him take nothing except bread to last until his next lodging. But if he asks for money, he is a false prophet. You shall not test or examine any prophet who speaks in the spirit. For every sin will be forgiven, but this sin will not be forgiven. But not everyone who speaks in the spirit is a prophet, but only if he has the ways of the Lord. So the false prophet and the prophet will be known by their ways. No prophet who orders a meal under the spirit's influence shall eat of it; if he does, he is a false prophet. Every prophet who teaches the truth, if he does not do what he teaches, is a false prophet. No prophet, tried and true, who does anything as an earthly symbol of the church, but does not teach others to do what he does, shall be judged among you, for he has his judgment with God, for the ancient prophets also did this. But whosoever says in the spirit, "Give me money," or something else, you shall not listen to him, but if he tells you to give for others who are in want, let no one judge him.

The criteria for distinguishing false from true prophecy in this passage have to do with self-gain and conduct, both fairly easy of application. Unfortunately the solution is not so simple as the three-day sojourn, asking for money or food under the spirit's seizure, or failure to live by the truth (whose version of it?) imply.

The problem of false prophecy appears in other early Christian literature, though not as extensively as in the Didache. The Shepherd of Hermas, Mand 11 1-14, denies the spirit to the false prophet, accuses him of speaking according to the desires of the inquirers, and states that his emptiness will be shown amid saints. False prophets are attacked in the letters of Ignatius (Eph 7, 9, 16 Phil 2 3 Smyr 4, 7), and in the writings of Origen (Contra Celsus 7, 9—11), Eusebius (Hist. Eccles. 3, 26), and Lucian (de morte Peregrini 11, 16)[7].

The Pseudo-Clementine literature suggests an even more simplistic approach to the problem of distinguishing false from true prophecy. According to the *Kerygmata Petrou*, "The whole of history runs in conjoined pairs (*suzugiai*), the first or left member of which represents false prophecy, the second or right member of which represents true prophecy."[8] The polemic against followers of John the Baptist has assumed the

---

[6] The Apostolic Fathers, 1950, 16.

[7] Bowlin, The Christian Prophets in the New Testament, 241—289.

[8] Cullmann, The Christology of the New Testament, 41.

form of decrying temporal priority, so that the mere fact that John preceded Jesus, the other member of the pair, suffices to identify him as false, along with Eve (the one exception), Ishmael, Esau, and Aaron.

In summary, the New Testament period bears witness to the continuing struggle to determine the genuine spokesman for God, testifies to a growing hostility toward false prophets, and attests a simplistic approach to the setting up of criteria for distinguishing true from false prophets.

# Excursus B: "'eṣā and dabar: The Problem of Authority/Certitude in Wisdom and Prophetic Literature"

The crisis that has struck at the very foundations of biblical theology was prompted in part by a failure to give more than a passing nod to wisdom literature, and has helped to create an atmosphere within which a careful look at wisdom is inevitable. Of course, other factors have turned the eyes of biblical scholars in this direction also, particularly the discovery and translation of numerous Mesopotamian and Egyptian collections, onomastica, as well as theological and sceptical parallels to the wisdom literature of the Old Testament. But more decisive than either the crisis in biblical theology or the excitement of new discovery has been the gradual erosion of the authority of holy writ, especially the prophetic claim to speak in the name of the Lord. Ours is an ethos in which it is no longer possible for many of us to accept the prophetic claim, *kō 'amăr 'ᵃdonay*, as anything more than human intuition couching itself in revelatory categories. To a generation for whom the transcendental world is sealed off from the one in which we are born, suffer and die, to use Anatole France's summary of human history, the arrogant boast, "Thus hath the Lord spoken", appeals far less than the ancient sage's "Listen, my son, to your father's advice." It is the supreme irony of our fate that at the same time that prophetic authority is being shown to have been minimal, that at no point can we dissect the divine word from the human,[1] the supposed secularity and non-authoritarian character of wisdom is rapidly giving way under attacks from all sides. In such a chaotic situation the time is ripe for a look at the problem of authority/certitude in wisdom and prophetic literature.

Nowhere is the issue stated more forcefully than in the article on the structure of Old Testament wisdom by W. Zimmerli in 1933.[2] Here the fundamental distinction between wisdom and prophecy stands out with special clarity and forcefulness: wisdom is anthropological, prophecy is theological. Or stated in another manner, wisdom is non-revelatory. Zimmerli's fundamental work discerns the inner ideological structure of wisdom, namely the desire to discover how to live the good life. He notes that the definitive question in wisdom is anthropological: "what is good/profitable *for man*?" For Zimmerli the avoidance of premature death is the supreme goal of man as seen from the eyes of the sage and to assist others in this fight to prolong and insure the good life wisdom *instructs, admonishes, states opinions* based on the sage's experiential research and rational power. Comparatives play a special role in the sage's pedagogy, according to Zimmerli, since man must be shown what is better for him. However, the counsel of the wise man is debatable, carrying with it *only the personal authority of the*

---

[1] O. Kaiser, Wort des Propheten und Wort Gottes, in: Tradition und Situation 75—92. For discussion of the crisis facing biblical theology, see Childs, Biblical Theology in Crisis.

[2] Zur Struktur der alttestamentlichen Weisheit 177—204.

*speaker*. Hence the response to *ʿeṣā* is understanding rather than obedience (as in the case of the *dabar* and *miṣwā*). Zimmerli writes that the sage could have said, "Fear God, *for he is your Creator*, for you are his creature, and such has he commanded!" Instead the wise man promised good health, plentiful food, and unobstructed paths! For the sage, then, man's possibilities rather than his duties were central.[3]

In a subsequent article[4] on "The Place and Limit of Wisdom in the Framework of Old Testament Theology" presented to the Colloque de Strasbourg May 17—19, 1962, Zimmerli returned to the non-authoritarian character of wisdom, although moderating his conclusions slightly: "Certainly we cannot say that counsel has no authority. It has the authority of insight. But that is quite different from the authority of the Lord, who decrees."[5] The motive clauses following admonitions are adduced as evidence for the radical distinction between the commandment of the law-giver and the admonition of the sage. Counsel thus affords a margin of liberty and proper decision, and the *yôʿeṣ* is one who seeks to persuade by the weight of his arguments and the evidence of his advice.

While this understanding of the structure of wisdom as anthropological, non-revelatory, non-authoritarian is expressed most forcefully by Zimmerli, it is by no means unique to him. It was, in fact, the fundamental clue that unlocked for J. Fichtner the key to the interpretation of Isaiah as a one-time sage who turned prophet.[6] Indeed for Fichtner the basic difference between wisdom and prophecy was "the nature of the authority with which they claim to speak." The presence of such terms as *tôrā*, *miṣwā* and *dabar* in wisdom constitutes no threat to this position, according to Fichtner, for "it can be proved with absolute certainty that the *termini* mentioned are never used with a legal significance (law, commandments) in the Proverbs, but everywhere with a significance which is in the context of wisdom (direction, advice)."[7]

As late as 1961 R. B. Y. Scott could write: "That priest and prophet were regarded as speaking with divine authority is clear. It is less certain that the same can be said of the 'counsel' of the wise man and of the elders."[8] Nevertheless, Scott does admit that a link between the sage and God is to be seen in the idea of wisdom as a gift from the Lord.[9] This notion had earlier been pursued by C. Rylaarsdam in the course of answering the question as to how one may hold together knowledge attained rationally

---

[3] Ibid. especially 181—189. 194—203 („Von Weisheitsgebot im strengen Sinn kann nicht geredet werden. Der autoritäre Charakter fehlt der Weisheitsmahnung, ihre Legitimation geschieht nicht durch Berufung auf irgendeine Autorität", 187).

[4] Ort und Grenze der Weisheit im Rahmen der alttestamentlichen Theologie 121—137.

[5] Ibid. 153. Zimmerli does, however, admit that wisdom within the context of scribal schools is authoritative and that personified wisdom in Prov 1—8 speaks with authority (Zur Struktur . . ., 182). But he argues that authority is personal, whereas wisdom appeals to impersonal experience (ibid. 187).

[6] Jesaja unter den Weisen, ThLZ 74 (1949), 75—80, reprinted in: Gottes Weisheit (1965), 18—26. For a recent treatment of the relationship of Isaiah to the scribal tradition, see W. Whedbee, Isaiah and Wisdom, 1968.

[7] Fichtner, Die altorientalische Weisheit in ihrer israelitisch-jüdischen Ausprägung, 1933, 83.

[8] Priesthood, Prophecy, Wisdom, and the Knowledge of God, JBL 80 (1961), 3.

[9] Ibid. 11. On this see also P. van Imschoot, Sagesse et esprit dans l'Ancien Testament, RB 47 (1938), 28f.

and through revelation.[10] Rylaarsdam arrives at a position that would minimize the differences between prophecy and wisdom; he does, however, deny that early wisdom (until Sirach and Wisdom of Solomon) had any place for grace.[11]

The distinction between early and late wisdom is fundamental to the interpretation of G. von Rad[12], who departs completely from the then-prevalent view that theological concern was alien to early wisdom. But while von Rad rejects the view that wisdom is strictly anthropological, he retains Zimmerli's thesis about its non-authoritative character. For von Rad wisdom's experiences always remain open to correction, are never brought to conclusion.[13] He quotes with approval Zimmerli's strong statement, "Such counsel does not demand obedience, but it asks to be tested: it appeals to the judgment of the hearer; it is intended to be understood, and to make decisions easier."[14] A change occurs, however, in Prov 1—9, so von Rad observes; here theological wisdom (in contrast to *Erfahrungsweisheit*) speaks with supreme authority, "has in it throughout something of an impatient ultimatum (1 20 8 3. 5)."[15] In connection with his attempt to prove that apocalyptic is an outgrowth of wisdom, a view that has been challenged recently by P. von der Osten-Sacken,[16] von Rad observed that wisdom loved to increase the weight of its insights by a prophetic manner of speech. Like Zimmerli, von Rad is astonished that the sages passed up their strongest argument for the legitimation of their summons (*Heilsgeschichte*) in favor of another, less obvious one, creation.[17]

Zimmerli's views about the non-authoritarian character of Israelite wisdom were not shared by everyone, however. J. Pedersen had time and again emphasized the authority of the *yôʿeṣ*, which he understood to mean "more than a proposal, something that is to be discussed."[18] Rather, counsel and action are taken to be identical, the prophet Isaiah even venturing to place both human and divine counsel in synonymous parallelism with works (Isa 5 19 29 15). Pedersen was even capable of speaking of *prophetic*, God-inspired counsel, as if there were no fundamental distinction between prophet and sage, at least along the lines of authority.[19] Similarly H. Gese insisted that prophet and sage alike spoke a word subject to the higher decision of God.[20] Admitting that in Egypt *Maʿat* was the norm (not the goal) of wisdom, Gese underscored the non-

---

[10] Revelation in Jewish Wisdom Literature, 1946. H. Schmid, Wesen und Geschichte der Weisheit, 199f. n. 286, perceives the significance of a commonality of ideas arrived at from the radically different avenues of prophet and sage.

[11] Rylaarsdam op. cit. passim.

[12] Old Testament Theology, I 1962, 418—459.

[13] Ibid. 422.

[14] Ibid. 434.

[15] Ibid. 443.

[16] Die Apokalyptik in ihrem Verhältnis zu Prophetie und Weisheit, 1969.

[17] Von Rad, Old Testament Theology, I 451f. It may be asked whether the imitation of prophetic speech patterns would increase the weight of the word of the sage. Such a conclusion is certainly not self-evident.

[18] Israel, I—II 1926, 128.

[19] Ibid. and III—IV 1940, 120f. On this see Wisd of Sol 7 27 (" . . . in every generation she [wisdom] passes into holy souls and makes them friends of God and prophets...") ; Sir 44 3f. II Esd 2 1, all of which are subsequent to the equation of torah and wisdom.

[20] Lehre und Wirklichkeit in der alten Weisheit, 1958, especially 45—50.

eudaemonistic and utilitarian nature of Israel's wisdom, the unique feature of which is the conviction that God determines *mišpat* and grants *ṣᵉdaqā* as *sovereign Lord.*

The "structure" supporting Zimmerli's position about wisdom's lack of authority began to give way with the sustained attack by B. Gemser[21]. Even the title of the article is influenced by Zimmerli: "The Spiritual Structure of Biblical Aphoristic Wisdom." Gemser submitted the root *ya'ăṣ* and its derivatives to close scrutiny, arguing that *'eṣā* has a strong element of authority on occasion (II Sam 16 23 Num 24 14 Isa 44 24 etc.), and that in Jer 18 8 and Ezek 7 26 there is scarcely any difference in authority between torah, word and counsel.[22] Gemser appealed to the basic role of *ṣᵉdaqā* in an impersonal yet authoritative world order (Gese) and to the hidden order already witnessed to in language itself (Jolles, von Rad). These factors, so he writes, assist us in answering the question, "Whence the authority of wisdom?" But if the word of priest, prophet and sage is alike authoritative, what distinguishes torah, word and counsel? Rylaarsdam's distinction of prophetic *outlook* as vertical, sage's as horizontal is approved by Gemser; thus the difference is perspective, not amount of authority. Gemser adds the coup de grâce; he asks why motive clauses appear in torah, word and counsel, concluding that they are mere pedagogic device, a method that led finally to Qoheleth. "The fear of the Lord is the beginning of wisdom"; this Gemser takes to be the keyword of Israel's wisdom.[23]

Gemser's frontal attack against Zimmerli's views received unexpected support from several quarters, the first by U. Skladny in the same year.[24] Skladny's study of the oldest collection of proverbs in Israel led him to reject Zimmerli's claim that Israelite wisdom was non-authoritarian. Appealing to H. Brunner's observation that in Egypt "Alle Weisheitslehren gründen ihren Anspruch auf die Autorität,"[25] Skladny contended that the absolute authority of Yahweh rests behind that of the wise; this is said to be illustrated by the emphasis upon human obligation and a world order that requires man to submit himself to it if he wishes to survive.[26] Since "Der Glaube an die von Gott gegebene Ordnung ist nicht nur Ornament, sondern Fundament, auf dem das Unternehmen der Weisheitslehrer ruht"[27] Skladny argued that the utilitarian emphasis attributed to wisdom was also misplaced, for the aim was to accord with the order God had provided for man's conduct, hence to discover and obey the will of God.[28] He concludes: "The attitude of unconditional submission to the absolute authority of Yahweh was the sole foundation of wisdom and at the same time of righteousness (and this surrender is ethical rather than pragmatic)."[29] Skladny thus underlined the proximity between wisdom and prophecy that Rylaarsdam and Gemser had noted.[30]

[21] The Spiritual Structure of Biblical Aphoristic Wisdom 3—10.

[22] Ibid. 144f. P. A. H. de Boer, The Counsellor, 42—71, had reached the same conclusion about the authority of counsel (particularly 56. 65. 71).

[23] Gemser op. cit. 146—149.

[24] Die ältesten Spruchsammlungen in Israel, 1962.

[25] H. Brunner, Die Weisheitsliteratur, HO I 2, 95.

[26] Skladny op. cit. 89f.

[27] E. Würthwein, Die Weisheit Ägyptens und das Alte Testament, 1959, 7.

[28] Skladny op. cit. 91.

[29] Ibid.

[30] Ibid. 92 ("Jahwe ist also auch für die ältere Weisheit der einen absoluten Authoritätsanspruch stellende souveräne Schöpfer und Herr der Welt und des Menschen

This problem-area of the relationship between prophet and wise man was scrutinized quite exhaustively by W. McKane in 1965.[31] His conclusion is that there was constant tension between the two since the wise men did not permit themselves the luxury of religious or ethical assumptions, their task being to advise the king on matters of statecraft.[32] McKane rejects the view that *ʿeṣā* was devoid of authority, especially as expressed by von Rad (advice on humdrum matters comparable in lack of authority to a judge's summing up to a jury).[33] Closer to the truth, in McKane's opinion, is M. Noth's observation that to neglect *ʿeṣa* is to expose oneself to the judgment of God.[34] The acid test of counsel is said to be the degree of success which it achieves when put into operation[35]; here McKane has subjected wisdom to the same criterion proposed by Deuteronomy for the prophetic word. The controversy in Jer 8 8f. is understood in terms of a genuine change in the function of the sage; McKane thinks of the latter as an apologist of the law, the new element being the sage's acceptance of the equation of torah and law.[36]

McKane's latest work, a massive commentary on Proverbs,[37] goes further in stressing the authoritative nature of ancient wisdom, particularly in Egypt. He observes that the hand of authority is heavy, but not dead, wisdom being necessary in the application of the counsels of the sages.[38] The authoritative character of the proverbial collections is enhanced, so McKane argues, by their language and style, particularly the imperatives and conditional clauses that define the circumstances in which the imperatives apply, as well as the motive clauses that recommend the imperatives and demonstrate their reasonableness, and the consequential clauses that show the effectiveness of the imperatives. McKane discerns in Egyptian wisdom literature a growing emphasis on authority, the Counsels of Wisdom reflecting an ascendancy of the element of command over that of argument.[39]

A pervasive Egyptian influence upon Israelite wisdom, particularly Pr 8, has been argued recently by C. Bauer-Kayatz.[40] She observes that the function of the fear of the Lord and the will of God shows clearly that wisdom instruction was not meant to be taken as non-obligatory counsel, but as a form of Yahweh's will carrying authority.[41] Furthermore, Bauer-Kayatz contends, wisdom's experiential foundation carries with it maximal authority, since the discovered order goes back to God, conveys his will, shares in his authority.[42] This store of knowledge is the product of many generations, and cannot be acquired without submission to the authority of elders, parents,

---

[vgl. besonders die Sammlung B], so daß die Weisheit damit in große Nähe zur prophetischen Vorstellungswelt rückt").

[31] Prophets and Wise Men. [32] Ibid. 48 and passim. [33] Ibid.

[34] Noth, Die Bewährung von Salomos „Göttlicher Weisheit", SVT 3 (1960), 236ff. According to Noth, Solomon's word is thought to have been superior to an oracle (232), so that the appeal to Solomon as the author of wisdom literature is in essence a search for additional authority. The Ahithophel narrative in II Sam 16 23 is very important to McKane's view about the authority of counsel.

[35] McKane op. cit. 56. 67. [36] Ibid. 106.

[37] Proverbs, 1970. [38] Ibid. 59.

[39] Ibid. 75—78. 119—121. 155.

[40] Einführung in die alttestamentliche Weisheit, 1969.

[41] Ibid. 33.

[42] Ibid. 34.

teachers and sages, and ultimately, God.[43] Bauer-Kayatz emphasizes Pr 1 20-33 3 13-20 8 as theological reflexion, Egyptian in orientation, in which wisdom speaks as a medium of revelation, legitimates her claim in terms of pre-existence (presence with God before creation), and warns that life and death are at stake, the way of wisdom becoming another option to obedience to the law. She concludes: "The purpose of all this wisdom theological reflexion is in the last resort to legitimate wisdom in its claim and promise, and place man in a decision situation over against its commandment of salvation"[44].

This brief survey of the course of scholarship in the field of wisdom literature indicates that the current flight to wisdom as more palatable to contemporary man may be as futile as Jonah's attempt to escape the Inevitable.[45] If in the area of authority wisdom differs little from prophecy, perhaps a second look at the authoritative character of the prophetic "spokesman of God" is in order.

It seems clear that in its earliest manifestation known to man prophecy was less authoritative than divination, the domain of the sage, at least if W. Moran is correct in his interpretation of the allusions in the Mari documents to taking an omen to see if the dream was seen.[46] The prophetic word is on occasion submitted to the judgment of the haruspex, the latter always carrying the final word.

Biblical prophecy appears to be different because of the apodictic nature of its language. But a closer look at the response to the prophets by those to whom the "authoritative" words were spoken proves how devoid of authority the prophetic message was, despite the claim that its origin was divine. We have seen that without exception the prophet was scorned and vilified, his words finding receptive minds only in a few "disciples" who preserved them until the course of history vindicated a message of doom. Where the prophets addressed themselves to the question of success the judgment is always the same, namely utter failure (thus Isaiah, Jeremiah, Ezekiel [and Amos]).

The same result is suggested by the frequency with which Disputations appear in prophetic literature. The nature and mood of these disputes prove that the prophet was engaged in a struggle for self-vindication, hence that his claim to be speaking for the deity did not go unchallenged. This is true even when the word of the prophet was favorable, for it is precisely in the majestic promises of Deutero-Isaiah that the controversy speeches dominate, playing a role second to none save hymn with divine self-asseveration. The presence of disputes in messages of weal and woe suggests that the prophets were aware that their words did not automatically carry authority, but had to be legitimated by persuasive argument. It is also likely, furthermore, that the call accounts are intended to serve as certification for the spoken word, although their value is severely limited because of the subjective character of each vision.

---

[43] Ibid. 40f.

[44] Ibid. 58ff., especially 95. For the "Before . . ." formula as a legitimation of authority, see Grapow, Die Welt vor der Schöpfung, ZÄS 67 (1931).

[45] For an attempt, legitimate in its own right, to comprehend the current relevance of wisdom to the theological curriculum, see W. Brueggemann, Happenings in Scripture Study and the Mood of Theological Education, Events Eight (Eden Theological Seminary Bulletin, 1968), no page numbers given.

[46] New Evidence from Mari on the History of Prophecy, Bib 50 (1969), 21—24, especially 24 note 2.

Again, the prophetic message itself is largely experiential and intuitive. None would deny the powerful role of the personality of the prophet in couching the poetic word in language that will communicate with his audience. Even if one chooses to believe that the ultimate source of the enigmatic revelatory word is divine, he must admit that this ecstatic, enigmatic word must then become a part of the prophet as he reflects upon it and interprets it for those of less spiritual perception.[47]

Prophetic texts on occasion also make it clear that certitude was not always present, that it was not always possible to tell whether a word had its origin in God or in the subconscious. One need only refer to Jeremiah's experience with his cousin Hanamel (32 6-8), where the appearance of Hanamel subsequent to a dream convinced the prophet that the vision had been sent by God, or again, to the confrontation with Hananiah, at which time Jeremiah did not know what God's word was. Likewise in I Kings 13 there is no certitude given the true prophet, so that he has no way of discerning who spoke the truth. In fact, our study of "false" prophecy indicated that no criterion is valid in distinguishing the true from the false prophet, so that each prophet must have struggled as much with his own doubts as with those who saw things differently.

If the usual assumption about prophecy's authority fares ill with closer inspection, what about the claim that wisdom is secular? Once again the claim cannot be defended. H. Schmid's fundamental study of "Righteousness as the Order of the World"[48] makes it abundantly clear that wisdom's point of departure was genuinely religious, that her world view was closely akin to that of prophecy and the Deuteronomic theologian. Wisdom was able to legitimate all claims in terms of the God who created the world so that obedience to the "laws" discovered by the sages was rewarded. This treasury of blessed knowledge, furthermore, was in the hands of representatives of the tradition, each sharing a portion of the authority of God. The sequence of authority included the king, particularly Solomon as the man especially endowed with the gift of wisdom, the elders, counsellors, and parents, both "Father" and "Mother" becoming technical terms in wisdom's vocabulary. Those who call attention to the special appeal of the teacher in terms of sonship have seldom noted that the authority of the father was not subject to discussion in ancient Israel. In his hands was the power over life and limb of the sons; hence the use of "my son" must not merely be viewed as a literary or pedagogic device. On the contrary, it communicated something of the authority of the teacher.[49]

The same sense of authority behind wisdom's teaching belongs to the twin ideas of the will of God and the fear of God, characteristic of Proverbs (and in the final form, at least, of Qoheleth). The sage was convinced that God's purpose had been made known in creation and that man's duty was to discover his will by submitting to the discipline of wisdom. Success in this endeavor could only be assured if one were conscious of God's freedom, that is, if he possessed fear of the Lord. Behind this conception is the idea of God's unknowability, the mystery within which the Creator hides himself.

[47] See especially Kaiser op. cit. 83ff.

[48] Gerechtigkeit als Weltordnung, 1968.

[49] If those scholars who understand *mašal* as a "ruling/power" word are correct, even this technical term alludes to the authority of the sage. See Bauer-Kayatz op. cit. 41; McKane, Proverbs, 22—33, rejects this meaning in favor of "model, exemplar, paradigm".

The hypostatization of wisdom in Pr 8 (and the use of the prophetic manner of speaking in Pr 2), despite the erotic prototype, functions almost like divine self-asseverations. Wisdom may invite men to her banquet table, but the context makes it plain that to refuse her invitation is to invite death. The voice of authority is heard in every syllable Dame Wisdom utters, for she is no ordinary street walker, and her food is better than bread and water. The supreme authority of wisdom is expressed in different fashion in Isaiah, where Yahweh is described as a Counsellor, even if ironically intended. But whether Dame Wisdom or Counsellor be the medium, the message is still thought to come from God himself, thus carrying the authority of the Sovereign of the universe.

The authoritative character of wisdom's claims is also evident from the motivation clauses by which she seeks to persuade to action. What is at stake here is life and death, so that one simply cannot afford to ignore her words. This fact is all the more decisive when one notes the individualistic presuppositions of wisdom. Since little comfort could be taken in corporate unity, wisdom demanded that every man determine his fate, although admitting in the end that even the best laid plans were subject to divine alteration. Just as the individualism of wisdom forbade the taking of comfort in the totality, so its universalism ruled out saving history as the content of motivation clauses. The role of creation faith in this respect must not be minimized, for it rests upon fundamental assumptions about the nature of the universe and the purpose of wisdom. In short, the Creator makes his will known in creation and by special endowment at subsequent periods, by the sage's counsel and the prophet's word, that is, and neither carries more authority than the other.

What, then, is to be said about the current trend in biblical studies to find a point of contact between modern man and wisdom as the hope of the future? Perhaps a glance at the history of wisdom will assist us in answering that question. Here one can discern a gradual trend toward dogma that finally gave birth to the scepticism of Qoheleth. Just as in prophecy the claims made in the name of the deity were not borne out in historical experience and resulted in the clash between true and false prophets that destroyed the movement, so in wisdom the authoritative assertions of one branch of wisdom created a crisis of confidence that split the movement in two directions, the sceptical and the dogmatic. It is ironical that Job, the great challenge to all dogma, is predicated on the assumption that God is just, and that its solution is a surrender to revelation. Small wonder that Sirach and Wisdom of Solomon have little difficulty in incorporating sacred history and torah into the wisdom tradition, for the authoritative character of counsel was there from the beginning. In short, between "Thus saith the Lord" and "Listen, my son, to your father's advice" there is no fundamental difference.[50]

---

[50] When a version of this discussion of *'eṣā* and *dabar* was read on October 23, 1970, in a Symposium on Wisdom Literature at the national meeting of the American Academy of Religion, meeting jointly with the Society of Biblical Literature and Society for the Scientific Study of Religion, R. Murphy insisted that the people who heard prophet and sage were aware of a difference in authority presupposed by the speakers. Murphy's helpful criticism calls attention to the fact that one must distinguish between the authority with which the prophet or sage thinks he speaks and the authority which the hearers are willing to grant the speaker. It is only when the two are at variance that conflict arises.

# Selected Bibliography

## *I. Works on False Prophecy*


Bacht, H., Wahres und falsches Prophetentum, Bib 32 (1951), 237—262.

Blank, S. H., Of a Truth the Lord Hath Sent Me: An Inquiry into the Source of the Prophet's Authority, 1955.

Buber, M., Falsche Propheten, Die Wandlung 2 (1946—47), 277—283.

Davidson, A. B., The False Prophets, Exp 2 (1895), 1—17.

Edelkoort, A. H., Prophet and Prophet, OTS 5 (1948), 179—189.

Halpern, E., Hosea 2: 1—3, A Quotation from the Words of False Prophets, Bet Miqra' 11 (1965—1966), 159—161 (Modern Hebrew).

Harms, Kl., Die falschen Propheten: Eine biblische Untersuchung, 1947.

Hempel, J., Vom irrenden Glauben, ZSystTh 7 (1930), 631—660.

Jacob, E., Quelques remarques sur les faux prophètes, ThZ 13 (1957), 479—486.

Kraus, H. J., Prophetie in der Krisis. Studien zu den Texten aus dem Buch Jeremia, 1964.

Matthes, J. C., The False Prophets of Israel, ModR 1884, 417—445.

Mowinckel, S., The "Spirit" and the "Word" in the Pre-Exilic Reforming Prophets, JBL 53 (1934), 199—227.

Osswald, E., Falsche Prophetie im Alten Testament, 1962.

—, Irrender Glaube in den Weissagungen der alttestamentlichen Propheten, WZJena, 1963, 65ff. (not available to the writer).

Overholt, T. W., Jeremiah 27—29: The Question of False Prophecy, JAAR 35 (1967), 241—249.

Quell, G., Wahre und falsche Propheten. Versuch einer Interpretation, 1952.

Rendtorff, R., Der wahre und der falsche Prophet im Deuteronomium, TWNT, hrsg. Rudolph Kittel, VI (1959), 807f.

Renner, J. T. E., False and True Prophecy, RefThR 25 (1966), 95—104.

Siegman, E. F., The False Prophets of the Old Testament, 1939.

Staerk, W., Das Wahrheitskriterion der alttestamentlichen Prophetie, ZSystTh 5 (1928), 76—101.

Stevenson, D. E., The False Prophet, 1965.

Tilson, E., False Prophets in the Old Testament, unpublished Ph. D. Dissertation, Vanderbilt University, 1951.

Von Rad, G., Die falschen Propheten, ZAW 51 (1933), 109—120.

Wolff, H. W., Hauptprobleme alttestamentlicher Prophetie, EvTh 15 (1955), 116—168.

—, Das Zitat im Prophetenspruch, BEvTh 4 (1937).

*II. General Works on Prophecy*

Anderson, B. W. and Harrelson, W. (eds.), Israel's Prophetic Heritage, Essays in Honor of James Muilenburg, 1962.

Albright, W. F., Samuel and the Beginnings of the Prophetic Movement, 1961.

Balla, E., Die Botschaft der Propheten, 1958.

Barth, K., Exegese von I Könige 13, 1955, also in: Church Dogmatics, II 2 1957.

Baumgartner, W., Die Auffassungen des 19. Jahrhunderts vom israelitischen Prophetismus, Archiv für Kulturgeschichte 15 (1922), 21—35, reprinted in: Zum Alten Testament und seiner Umwelt, 1959, 27—41.

Begrich, J., Studien zu Deuterojesaja, 1963.

Buber, M., The Prophetic Faith, 1949.

Childs, B., Isaiah and the Assyrian Crisis, 1967.

Clements, R. E., The Conscience of the Nation, 1967.

—, Prophecy and Covenant, 1965.

Crenshaw, J. L., Amos and the Theophanic Tradition, ZAW 80 (1968), 203—215.

—, The Influence of the Wise upon Amos, ZAW 79 (1967), 42—52.

—, A Liturgy of Wasted Opportunity: Am 4 6-12 Isa 9 7–10 4 5 25-29, Sem 1 (1970), 27—37.

—, Method in Determining Wisdom Influence upon "Historical" Literature, JBL 88 (1969), 129—142.

—, Popular Questioning of the Justice of God in Ancient Israel, ZAW 82 (1970), 380—395.

—, YHWH Ṣᵉbaʼôt Šᵉmô: A Form-Critical Analysis, ZAW 81 (1969), 156—175.

De Vaux, R., Jerusalem and the Prophets, 1965.

Duhm, B., Israels Propheten, 1922².

Eißfeldt, O., The Prophetic Literature, in: The Old Testament and Modern Study, edited by H. H. Rowley, 1961 (originally 1951), 115—161.

Elliger, K., Kleine Schriften zum Alten Testament, 1966.

Fichtner, J., Propheten II B. Seit Amos, RGG V (1961), 619—627.

Fohrer, G. (mit Galling, K.)., Ezechiel, 1955.

Fohrer, G., Die Propheten des Alten Testaments im Blickfeld neuer Forschung, in: Studien zur alttestamentlichen Prophetie, 1967, 1—17.

—, Remarks on Modern Interpretation of the Prophets, JBL 80 (1961), 309—319.

—, Zehn Jahre Literatur zur alttestamentlichen Prophetie, ThR 28 (1961—62), 1—75. 235—297. 301—374.

Frost, S., Patriarchs and Prophets, 1963.

Gottwald, N. K., All the Kingdoms of the Earth, 1964.

Gray, J., I & II Kings, 1963.

Gunneweg, A. H. J., Mündliche und schriftliche Tradition der vorexilischen Prophetenbücher als Problem der neueren Prophetenforschung, 1959.

Hammershaimb, E., Some Aspects of Old Testament Prophecy from Isaiah to Malachi, 1966.

Hentschke, R., Die Stellung der vorexilischen Schriftpropheten zum Kultus, 1957.

Hermann, S., Die prophetischen Heilserwartungen im Alten Testament, 1965.

Heschel, A., The Prophets, 1962.

Hesse, F., Das Verstockungsproblem im Alten Testament, 1955.

Hillers, D. R., Treaty-Curses and the Old Testament Prophets, 1964.
Horst, F., Gottes Recht, 1961.
Hyatt, J. P., Prophetic Religion, 1947.
—, The Prophetic Criticism of Israelite Worship, 1963.
Jacob, E., Le prophétisme israélite d'après les recherches récents, RHPR 32 (1952), 59—69.
Kaufmann, Y., The Religion of Israel, 1960.
Klopfenstein, M. A., I Könige 13, in: ΠΑΡΡΗΣΙΑ, Karl Barth zum achtzigsten Geburtstag, 1966, 639—672.
Kuhl, C., The Prophets of Israel, 1960.
Lindblom, J., Prophecy in Ancient Israel, 1962.
Lods, A., The Prophets and the Rise of Judaism, 1937.
McKane, W., Prophets and Wise Men, 1965.
Mowinckel, S., Prophecy and Tradition, 1946.
Muilenburg, J., The "Office" of the Prophet in Ancient Israel, in: The Bible in Modern Scholarship, edited by J. P. Hyatt, 1965, 74—97.
Napier, B. D., Prophets in Perspective, 1962—1963.
Nielsen, E., Oral Tradition, 1954.
Noth, M., Könige, 1967 ff.
—, The Laws in the Pentateuch and Other Essays, 1966.
Porteous, N. W., Living the Mystery, 1967.
Rendtorff, R., Erwägungen zur Frühgeschichte des Prophetentums in Israel, ZThK 59 (1962), 145—167.
—, Men of the Old Testament, 1968.
—, Tradition und Prophetie, ThVia, 8 (1962), 216—226.
Rendtorff, R. und Koch, K. (hrsg.), Studien zur Theologie der alttestamentlichen Überlieferungen (Festschrift für G. von Rad), 1961.
Ringgren, H., Israelite Religion, 1966.
Robinson, T. H., Prophecy and the Prophets in Ancient Israel, 1923.
Rowley, H. H., From Moses to Qumran, 1963.
—, Men of God, 1963.
—, The Nature of Old Testament Prophecy in the Light of Recent Study, HThR 38 (1945), 1—38.
—, The Servant of the Lord, 1952.
— (ed.), Studies in Old Testament Prophecy (Th. Robinson Festschrift), 1957.
Rudolph, W., Jeremia, 1958.
Sachsse, E., Die Propheten des Alten Testaments und ihre Gegner, Zeit- und Streitfragen des Glaubens der Weltanschauung und Bibelforschung, 1919.
Scharbert, J., Das Entstehen der prophetischen Bücher, in: Bibel und zeitgemäßer Glaube, hrsg. K. Schubert, 1965, 193—237.
—, Die Propheten Israels bis 700 v. Chr., 1965.
Scott, R. B. Y., The Relevance of the Prophets, 1953 (revised 1968).
Vawter, B., The Conscience of Israel, 1961.
Von Rad, G., The Message of the Prophets, 1968.
—, Old Testament Theology, I/II, 1962/1965.
—, The Problem of the Hexateuch and Other Essays, 1966.

Vriezen, T. C., The Religion of Ancient Israel, 1967.

Westermann, C., Basic Forms of Prophetic Speech, 1967.

—, Forschung am Alten Testament, 1964.

—, Propheten, Biblisch-Historisches Handwörterbuch, hrsg. Reicke, B. und Rost, L., III 1966, 1496—1512.

Whitley, C. F., The Prophetic Achievement, 1963.

Wildberger, H., Jesaja, 1965ff.

Wolff, H. W., Gesammelte Studien zum Alten Testament, 1964.

Würthwein, E. und Kaiser, O. (hrsg.), Tradition und Situation, Studien zur alttestamentlichen Prophetie (Festschrift für A. Weiser), 1963.

Zimmerli, W., Ezechiel, 1962ff.

—, Gottes Offenbarung, Gesammelte Aufsätze, 1963.

—, The Law and the Prophets, 1965.

# A. Index of Authors

# B. Index of Scripture

*a. Canonical Literature*

Gen



Ex



Lev



Num



Deut



Josh



Judg



I Sam

*b. Extra-canonical Literature*



# C. Index of Hebrew Words

## Beihefte
## zur Zeitschrift für die alttestamentliche Wissenschaft

Herausgegeben von GEORG FOHRER

---

Zuletzt erschienen:

Yariḫ und Nikkal und der Preis der Kuṯarāt-Göttinnen. Ein kultisch-magischer Text aus Ras Schamra. Von W. HERRMANN. X, 48 Seiten. Mit 1 Tafel. 1968. DM 18,— (Heft 106)

The Samaritan Chronicle No. II (or: Sepher Ha-Yamim) From Josua to Nebuchadnezzar. By J. MACDONALD. VIII, 227, 93 Seiten. 1969. Ganzleinen DM 70,— (Heft 107)

The Problem of Etiological Narrative in the Old Testament. By B. O. LONG. VIII, 94 Seiten. 1968. Ganzleinen DM 24,— (Heft 108)

Ursprünge und Strukturen alttestamentlicher Eschatologie. Von H.-P. MÜLLER. XII, 232 Seiten. 1969. Ganzleinen DM 46,— (Heft 109)

Mose. Überlieferung und Geschichte. Von H. SCHMID. VIII, 113 Seiten. 1968. Ganzleinen DM 32,— (Heft 110)

The Prophetic Word of Hosea. A Morphological Study. By M. J. BUSS. XIV, 142 Seiten. 1969. Ganzleinen DM 46,— (Heft 111)

Text und Textform im hebräischen Sirach. Untersuchungen zur Textgeschichte und Textkritik der hebräischen Sirachfragmente aus der Kairoer Geniza. Von H. P. RÜGER. VIII, 117 Seiten. 1970. Ganzleinen DM 46,— (Heft 112)

Die Wurzel schalom im Alten Testament. Von W. EISENBEIS. XVI, 367 Seiten. 1969. Ganzleinen DM 80,— (Heft 113)

Das Todesrecht im Alten Testament. Studien zur Rechtsform der Mot-Jumat-Sätze. Von H. SCHULZ. X, 208 Seiten. 1969. Ganzleinen DM 42,— (Heft 114)

Studien zur alttestamentlichen Theologie und Geschichte (1949—1966). Von G. FOHRER. X, 371 Seiten. 1969. Ganzleinen DM 74,— (Heft 115)

Prophet und Tradition. Versuch einer Problemstellung. Von M. L. HENRY. X, 77 Seiten. 1970. Ganzleinen DM 22,— (Heft 116)

Die Psalmen: Stilistische Verfahren und Aufbau. Mit besonderer Berücksichtigung von Ps 1—41. Von N. H. RIDDERBOS. Aus dem Holländischen von K. E. MITTRING. Etwa 320 Seiten. 1970. Ganzleinen etwa DM 40,— (Heft 117)

Strukturen und Figuren im Kult von Jerusalem. Studien zur altorientalischen, vor- und frühisraelitischen Religion. Von F. STOLZ. XI, 235 Seiten. 1970. Ganzleinen DM 58,— (Heft 118)

Geschichtliche Rückblicke und Motive in der Prophetie des Amos, Hosea und Jesaja. Von J. VOLLMER. X, 217 Seiten. 1970. Ganzleinen DM 62,— (Heft 119)

Die Priesterschrift von Numeri 1, 1 bis 10, 10 — literarkritisch und traditionsgeschichtlich untersucht. Von D. KELLERMANN, VI, 168 Seiten. 1970. Ganzleinen DM 48,— (Heft 120)

Ezechiel und Deuterojesaja. Berührungen in der Heilserwartung der beiden großen Exilspropheten. Von D. BALTZER. XX, 193 Seiten. 1971. Ganzleinen DM 58,— (Heft 121)

Untersuchungen zur sogenannten Baruchschrift. Von GUNTHER WANKE. XII, 156 Seiten. 1971. Ganzleinen DM 42,— (Heft 122)

Vorformen der Schriftexegese innerhalb des Alten Testaments. Untersuchungen zum literarischen Werden der auf Amos, Hosea und Micha zurückgehenden Bücher im hebräischen Zwölfprophetenbuch. Von I. WILLI-PLEIN. Etwa 304 Seiten. 1971. Etwa DM 88,— (Heft 123)

Walter de Gruyter · Berlin · New York